on track ...

The Doobie Brothers

every album, every song

Andrew Wild

sonicbondpublishing.com

Sonicbond Publishing Limited
www.sonicbondpublishing.co.uk
Email: info@sonicbondpublishing.co.uk

First Published in the United Kingdom 2026
First Published in the United States 2026

British Library Cataloguing in Publication Data:
A Catalogue record for this book is available from the British Library

ISBN 978-1-78952-462-8

Typeset in ITC Garamond & ITC Avant Garde
Printed and bound in England

Graphic design and typesetting: Full Moon Media

Follow us on social media:

Twitter: https://twitter.com/SonicbondP
Instagram: https://www.instagram.com/sonicbondpublishing_/
Facebook: https://www.facebook.com/SonicbondPublishing/

Linktree QR code:

Also by Andrew Wild

Local History

108 Steps Around Macclesfield (Sigma Press, 1994 / 2nd edition,
Rumble Strips, 2018: out of print)
Exploring Chester (Sigma Press, 1996 / re-publication, Rumble Strips, 2018: out of print)
Ever Forward (MADS, 1997: out of print)

Biographies

Play On: The Authorised Biography Of Twelfth Night (Twelfth Night, 2009: out of print)
One For The Record: The Authorised Biography Of Galahad
(Avalon, 2013 / 2nd edition, 2018 / 3rd edition 2026)
His Love: Art, Music And Faith – The Authorised Biography Of Geoff Mann (Sonicbond, 2023)

Books About Music

Pink Floyd Song By Song (Fonthill, 2017)
Queen On Track (Sonicbond, 2018)
The Beatles: An A-Z Guide To Every Song (Sonicbond, 2019: out of print)
Solo Beatles 1969-1980 On Track (Sonicbond, 2020)
Crosby, Stills And Nash On Track (Sonicbond, 2020)
Dire Straits On Track (Sonicbond, 2021)
Fleetwood Mac In The 1970s (Sonicbond, 2021)
Eric Clapton Solo On Track (Sonicbond, 2021)
Eric Clapton Sessions (Sonicbond, 2022)
Phil Collins In The 1980s (Sonicbond, 2022)
The Allman Brothers Band On Track (Sonicbond, 2022)
A Mirror Of Dreams: The Progressive Rock Revival 1981 To 1983 (Kingmaker, 2024)
Live Aid: The Greatest Show On Earth (Sonicbond, 2024)
Four Sides Of The Circle: The Beatles: Every Song, Every Take, Every Mix,
Every Release 1957-2023 (Rumble Strips, 2024)
The Beatles On Track 1962-1966 (with Alberto Bravin) (Sonicbond, 2025)
A Playground Of Broken Hearts: The Progressive Rock Revival 1984 To 1989 (Kingmaker, 2025)
Apple Of My Eye: The Story Of Apple Records And The End Of The Beatles (Sonicbond, 2025)
The Beautiful South + The Housemartins On Track (Sonicbond, 2026)

Books About Films

James Bond On Screen (Sonicbond, 2021)

Books About Comics

The Perfect Marvel Comics Collection 1939-1985 (Rumble Strips, 2022: out of print)

Plays

The Difficult Crossing (Stagescripts, 2016)
A Difficult Man (Rumble Strips, 2021: out of print)

Would you like to write for Sonicbond Publishing?

At Sonicbond Publishing we are always on the look-out for authors, particularly for our two main series:

On Track. Mixing fact with in depth analysis, the On Track series examines the work of a particular musical artist or group. All genres are considered from easy listening and jazz to 60s soul to 90s pop, via rock and metal.

On Screen. This series looks at the world of film and television. Subjects considered include directors, actors and writers, as well as entire television and film series. As with the On Track series, we balance fact with analysis.

While professional writing experience would, of course, be an advantage the most important qualification is to have real enthusiasm and knowledge of your subject. First-time authors are welcomed, but the ability to write well in English is essential.

Sonicbond Publishing has distribution throughout Europe and North America, and all books are also published in E-book form. Authors will be paid a royalty based on sales of their book.

Further details are available from www.sonicbondpublishing.co.uk. To contact us, complete the contact form there or email info@sonicbondpublishing.co.uk

on track ...

The Doobie Brothers

Contents

Introduction

The Doobie Brothers hold a unique place in American music history. Their original sound – which blended boogie rock and folk-blues with hints of country-rock and a powerful rhythm section – was harmonically rich and supremely commercial. Songs like 'China Grove' and 'Long Train Runnin'' and, especially, 'Listen To The Music' captured the essence of early-1970s American rock. The Doobies' songs were melodic and accessible but also, when needed, hard and exciting.

Their secret weapon was Patrick Simmons, the only constant member. Simmons, born in upstate Washington but raised in San Jose, was a vital, often underappreciated, creative force within The Doobie Brothers. His roots in country, folk and fingerstyle guitar traditions brought a gentle intricacy to the band's sound. He served as a key stabilising figure during the band's many transitions.

In their early years, the blend of Simmons' love of Americana, Appalachian folk and New Orleans-style rhythms with Tom Johnston's loud, bluesy, driving rhythm guitar gave the Doobie Brothers a uniquely eclectic identity. The commercial sheen of their music placed them as one of a number of acts that helped define the 'California sound' of the early 1970s. But whereas The Eagles, Crosby Stills & Nash, Jackson Browne and the rest tended towards the homogenous, The Doobies' very diverse musical palette positioned them towards the left field with fellow radicals such as Little Feat and Steely Dan.

The recruitment of former Steely Dan vocalist/keyboardist Michael McDonald in 1975 fundamentally shifted the band's focus and artistic direction. With his distinctive, soulful voice and jazz-influenced keyboard playing, McDonald steered the Doobie Brothers toward a more polished, R&B-inflected pop sound. Their albums, like *Takin' It To The Streets* and *Minute By Minute,* incorporated elements of soul and funk and bore some of the group's biggest commercial hits, notably 'What A Fool Believes', which won multiple Grammys. As the group leaned into McDonald's soul-pop direction, Pat Simmons continued to contribute his distinctively earthy, folk-inflected material. The Doobie Brothers' original spirit, rooted in backwoods storytelling, was never entirely lost.

This transition alienated some long-time fans who missed the raw, guitar-driven rock of the Tom Johnston era. The shift created a lasting schism in the fan base and an ongoing debate about the band's true identity: in reality, they never had a clear identity or a fixed sound. They employed seven lead singers in their career: notably, of course, Tom Johnston, Pat Simmons and Michael McDonald, but Cornelius Bumpus, Keith Knudsen, Tiran Porter and John McFee sang lead on at least one song in their back catalogue. This diversity was both a strength – they were always open to any type of musical expression within the band – but also a frustration to fans who wanted endless reruns of 'China Grove'.

The band split in 1982, but reformed a few years later, reuniting their first commercially successful lineup. Their albums and concert tours for the next 30 years focused on the 1971-1975 oeuvre, but with new songs such as feel-good 'The Doctor' with Tom Johnston's energetic voice to the fore. Michael McDonald re-joined permanently in 2021.

The Doobie Brothers' impact on American music lies in their versatility and resilience: the pre-McDonald era provided a blueprint for blue-collar American rock, while the later years showcased an ability to adapt and thrive in the more refined landscape of late-1970s pop. This cross-genre appeal has made The Doobie Brothers one of the most enduring and influential American rock bands of the 20th century.

Unless stated otherwise, quotes from Pat Simmons and Tom Johnston are taken from *Long Train Runnin': Our Story*; quotes from Michael McDonald from *What A Fool Believes: A Memoir*; and quotes from other band members from *The Doobie Brothers: Behind The Scenes With Today's Hottest Group.*

Opening Thoughts: The Doobie Brothers And The Sound Of 1970s America

The 1970s occupy a peculiar position in the history of American music. Sandwiched between the countercultural tumult of the 1960s and the corporatised entertainment landscape of the 1980s, the decade was marked by a paradoxical mix of experimentation and consolidation. Genres blurred, industry structures hardened and the audience diversified – both demographically and geographically.

In the political realm, the US was undergoing a painful reassessment of its own identity. The drawn-out end to the Vietnam War eroded public trust in government. Watergate amplified a cynicism that filtered into art and popular discourse. Economically, the oil crisis of 1973 and stagflation dampened post-war optimism. Yet within music, these same years offered fertile ground for hybrid forms and for bands willing to straddle – or defy – stylistic boundaries.

California emerged as a particularly influential hub in this landscape. While the Laurel Canyon scene in Los Angeles projected a sun-kissed folk-rock idealism through artists like Jackson Browne, The Eagles and Linda Ronstadt, the San Francisco Bay Area bred an edgier eclecticism – Santana's Latin-rock fusion, the Grateful Dead's improvisational jams and Tower of Power's horn-driven funk all flourished here. Into this environment came The Doobie Brothers: neither purely of the LA school nor entirely of the Bay's psychedelic lineage, but a synthesis of multiple traditions, tied together by a professionalism and melodic directness that made them palatable to AM radio without sacrificing musicianship.

When The Doobie Brothers formed in 1970, they were part of a second wave of Californian rock bands who had absorbed the innovations of the late 1960s but were not bound to psychedelic excess. Their early sets in San Jose clubs drew on blues, folk and R&B covers, alongside original material rooted in working-class experience.

The group's emergence coincided with a crucial technological and commercial shift: the expansion of FM radio. Unlike AM's three-minute single orientation, FM album-oriented rock stations could play longer tracks, sequence deep cuts and give exposure to more complex arrangements. This allowed bands like The Doobies to present multiple sides of their identity – from tight, radio-friendly singles to extended jams.

While Los Angeles songwriters were often characterised by an acoustic introspection, Northern California bands embraced rhythmic variety. This made The Doobies kin to Little Feat (formed in Los Angeles but having a sideways approach to composition and performance) with a bold willingness to draw from New Orleans funk, country and blues shuffles, rather than commit solely to the Crosby, Stills & Nash/Seals & Croft/James Taylor/Eagles/Bread/Captain & Tenille template.

The American rock ecosystem of the 1970s was an unusually permeable environment. Studio musicians moved freely between projects, producers worked across genres and touring bills often paired seemingly dissimilar acts – leading to a cross-pollination of ideas that would be far rarer in later decades. The Doobie Brothers were prime beneficiaries of this climate.

The most obvious personnel overlap came with guitarist Jeff 'Skunk' Baxter, who moved from Steely Dan to The Doobies in 1974. Baxter brought with him an ear for jazz-influenced chord voicings and rhythmic subtleties learned in the meticulous studio environment of Steely Dan's early albums. This influence was felt almost immediately: while the Tom Johnston-Pat Simmons core had thrived on tight, interlocking rhythm guitars and straightforward harmonic structures, Baxter encouraged richer arrangements, more exploratory solos and expanded tonal palettes.

In Steely Dan's case, the link to The Doobie Brothers was as much philosophical as musical. Both bands, by the late 1970s, embraced meticulous studio craft and a willingness to employ top-tier session players. Steely Dan, however, retreated entirely from touring after 1974, whereas The Doobies thrived as a live act. This difference in strategy ensured that The Doobies maintained a strong grassroots following, even as their sound became more polished.

The Steely Dan connection also extended to Michael McDonald, who had been part of that band's touring lineup before joining The Doobies. His vocal phrasing and keyboard textures bore the unmistakable stamp of Donald Fagen and Walter Becker's harmonic sensibilities. When he joined The Doobie Brothers in 1975, he brought that vocabulary wholesale – the ii-V-I turnarounds, the suspended chords and the tight, voice-led keyboard parts – all of which would reshape the band's sound in the second half of the decade.

The mid-1970s were a moment of flux for rock bands across the spectrum. Singer-songwriters were ceding radio space to disco, and funk was climbing the charts alongside a resurgent interest in jazz-fusion. For The Doobie Brothers, Tom Johnston's health issues provided both a challenge and an opportunity. Johnston, the architect of their early guitar-driven hits, was forced to scale back his involvement during the 1975-76 period. In his absence, the band recruited Michael McDonald.

Takin' It To The Streets (1976) was the first full flowering of this new approach. Tracks like the title song replaced the earthy drive of 'Rockin' Down the Highway' with a laid-back, syncopated groove anchored by McDonald's Fender Rhodes. Lyrically, McDonald's compositions tended toward introspection and urban imagery, contrasting with Johnston's and Simmons' more rural storytelling. The album also contained 'Wheels Of Fortune', a reminder that the folk-country strain had not been abandoned entirely.

The commercial breakthrough came with *Minute By Minute* (1978). The record's centrepiece, 'What A Fool Believes', co-written by McDonald and

Kenny Loggins, fused jazz-inflected harmony with a pop melody so accessible that it topped the *Billboard* Hot 100 and won three Grammys, including Record of the Year. Other tracks like 'Dependin' On You' retained Simmons' voice in the mix, maintaining a balance between the band's past and present.

For some fans, however, this period represented a loss of the rough-and-ready charm that had characterised early albums like *Toulouse Street* (1972) and *The Captain And Me* (1973). This tension – between the visceral appeal of the Johnston/Simmons guitar era and the urbane sophistication of the McDonald-led lineup – has become one of the defining debates in Doobie fandom.

Little Feat's piano player, Bill Payne, would contribute to many of The Doobie Brothers' early albums. Operating largely outside the pop mainstream, Little Feat embodied a 'musician's musician' ethos. Albums like *Dixie Chicken* (1973) showcased their groove-driven eclecticism, which mirrored Pat Simmons' interests within The Doobie Brothers. Little Feat's Lowell George, a slide guitar master who had cut his teeth in Frank Zappa's Mothers of Invention, was another fellow traveller in this world. Little Feat's syncopated funk-rock grooves, indebted to New Orleans R&B pioneers like The Meters, paralleled Patrick Simmons' taste for Southern rhythmic feels – a connection that would surface in Doobie tracks like 'Neal's Fandango' and 'South City Midnight Lady', both of which use rhythmic push-pull in a way far more complex than standard California rock fare. Yet, Little Feat's sales never matched The Doobies'. The contrast illustrates how even musically adventurous acts could capture mass audiences if they married experimentation to melodic immediacy – something The Doobies managed more consistently.

In scholarly terms, The Doobie Brothers, Steely Dan and Little Feat participated in a 1970s trend toward genre hybridity and professionalised musicianship, but The Doobies uniquely combined those qualities with a populist, tour-driven work ethic.

Their split in 1982 might have been the final chapter for many bands, but The Doobie Brothers' 1987 reunion demonstrated both the enduring affection of their audience and the adaptability of their catalogue. The set lists leaned heavily on the Johnston/Simmons years, reaffirming their roots-rock credentials. The 1989 album *Cycles* produced 'The Doctor', a track that sounded, in arrangement and energy, like it could have been recorded in 1973. It was a top ten hit single.

Over the next three decades, The Doobies balanced nostalgia with incremental evolution. They occasionally flirted with contemporary production values, as on 2000's *Sibling Rivalry*, but generally preserved the warmth and drive of their 1970s sound. Tours frequently paired them with acts from their heyday, creating live bills that mirrored the eclecticism of 1970s festival lineups. Michael McDonald's return in 2021 symbolically reunited the two dominant eras of the band's history, allowing them to present their full range of music in a single concert. Their latest album, 2025's *Walk This Road*, has a claim to be one of their best.

Even after more than 50 years, The Doobie Brothers' influence is evident in multiple musical currents. Americana and country rock acts like Zac Brown Band adopt the Doobies' blend of acoustic roots with rhythmic sophistication. Groups such as Tedeschi Trucks Band mirror the interplay of multiple guitarists and rhythmic looseness seen in early Doobies. The McDonald era's polished grooves have been rediscovered by a younger audience, spurred by irony-tinged but genuine appreciation for the 'Yacht Rock' craftsmanship of the late 1970s.

The Doobie Brothers' trajectory is inseparable from the broader story of 1970s American music. They emerged from a fertile regional scene, embraced cross-genre influences, navigated a dramatic stylistic transformation and maintained both commercial viability and artistic credibility. In the end, their legacy lies not only in hits like 'Listen To The Music', 'Black Water' or 'What A Fool Believes' but in the way they modelled resilience, openness to change and the value of keeping one foot in the grassroots even as the other explores new terrain.

They're still walking that road.

We were a work in progress all the time. We had Pat's finger picking, we had my rhythm, we had rock 'n' roll. So we would venture into all three of those arenas and try stuff. It was a lot of fun.
Tom Johnston, interviewed by *Guitar Player* (2024)

A lot of people have credited me with – or accused me of – single-handedly changing the band's sound. But my take on that is it mostly had to do with the conspicuous void left by Tom's departure. From the beginning, the band, as it was, with Tom and Pat being the main writers, created a fairly eclectic and diverse songbook, experimenting in everything from psychedelic folk rock and slack-key instrumentals to funk blues rock. Now, in Tom's absence, all the band members ... in their own way, out of necessity, contributed something to this new scattering of musical directions.
Michael McDonald quoted in *What A Fool Believes: A Memoir* (2024)

As for the music, that's constantly in flux; you're constantly working with it. As musicians, I feel anybody who plays with this band, or even comes to play only for a short period of time, has complete freedom to express their musical viewpoint. We don't say, 'Hey now, wait a minute, that doesn't fit the Doobie Brothers sound', or anything.
Pat Simmons, quoted in *The Doobie Brothers: Behind The Scenes With Today's Hottest Group* (1980)

The Doobie Brothers (1971)

Personnel:
Tom Johnston: vocals, guitars, harmonica, piano
Patrick Simmons: vocals, guitars
Dave Shogren: bass, organ, backing vocals
John Hartman: drums, tambourine
Recorded at Pacific Recording, San Mateo, California, between November and December 1970
Produced by Lenny Waronker and Ted Templeman
Released: April 1971
Charts: did not chart

Before the hit singles, platinum records and stadium tours, there was *The Doobie Brothers* – an unassuming debut that came and went with barely a ripple in 1971. Here was the sound of a band still figuring itself out.

The Doobie Brothers were formed in September 1970 in San Jose, California, as a quartet: Tom Johnston (vocals, guitar), Patrick Simmons (guitar, vocals), Dave Shogren (bass) and John Hartman (drums). After playing clarinet in his high school band, Tom Johnston started to learn the guitar at the age of 12, inspired by the blues, R&B and rock 'n' roll records of his older brother. He played in rock groups in high school and college (an art major at San Jose State), as well as in a local working band called The Charades. 'This band was my first experience playing specifically soul music', he writes in his memoirs. 'Singing backgrounds and a couple of lead vocals on songs I wrote for all-Black audiences. It was an education and experience you couldn't get in Visalia [Johnston's hometown, an agricultural city 40 miles from Fresno]. As a freshman in high school, my life changed when I saw James Brown in nearby Fresno. It was a classic soul revue show... I was knocked out! He was electrifying.' Johnston's sound was also heavily influenced by the loud guitar-based music of Cream, The Jimi Hendrix Experience and Mountain. Soon, he joined The Implicits, recording two of his original songs in Los Angeles in 1965: 'Give Me Justice' and 'She's Alright'. These were released on Atoll Records.

Meanwhile, Pat Simmons was inspired to pick up the guitar by a friend. 'We moved to a new neighbourhood in Los Gatos', he said in 2011. 'He invited me over one afternoon. His mother had a Harmony archtop – she and his dad had a country band. It was a nicer model, with a glossy finish. And I flipped when I saw it – an instrument I'd seen Ricky Nelson, Elvis and Chuck Berry play on television. I put it on my knee, and he taught me a G chord. After that, I had an *incredible* desire to play guitar. I'd go to his house every day.' He took guitar lessons 'from a lady in San Jose who was a traditional folk player. At her house, I saw a stereo system made from a kit her husband assembled. And she had Josh White, Pete Seeger and Appalachian folk records.' He was soon listening to the likes of Joan Baez, Pete Seeger, Odetta and Bob Dylan and reading the beat poets, Allen Ginsberg and Neal Cassady.

'For me, it felt like a counterculture soundtrack', he wrote. 'A sonic uprising. I felt inspired and transported. I loved folk music and obscure Appalachian songs. I absorbed all of that incredible American music as a teenager and decided that's what I wanted to play.'

He formed a duo with a friend and played pick-up gigs in a coffeehouse in Saratoga. After a meeting with Jorma Kaukonen, later with Jefferson Airplane, Simmons was inspired to play in local bands, covering everything from folk blues to electric psychedelic… the British Invasion. Because of how conservative my family was, I was not allowed to play in rock 'n' roll bands, so I had to sneak out to do it.'

Simmons left home, dropped LSD and enrolled at San Jose State University, studying psychology and playing gigs with a group called Scratch. Tom Johnston also settled in San Jose, playing in a couple of bands, picking up some solo acoustic gigs and working construction to pay the rent. He was introduced to Skip Spence, the troubled-but-brilliant founder of Moby Grape. Spence and Johnston jammed with other musicians, including a bass player called Dave Shogren and drummer John Hartman.

In March 1970, Johnston and Hartman formed a trio called Pud with bassist Greg Murphy. Pud gigged regularly and took part in recording sessions produced by Skip Spence. 'Pud was kind of a transformational band', Johnston told *Vintage Guitar* in 2011. 'One week, we'd play power-trio stuff like Cream or Mountain, and the next, we'd be playing soul with background singers and a horn section. It was all over the map, with different players every week except for John Hartman and me. It's amazing how much happened in a short period – how many bands, how many gigs, how many musicians I met. It all happened while I was an art major at San Jose State and wound up living at 285 South 12th Street, which was kind of a musical center for San Jose. It didn't matter if they played B-3 or drums, guitar, bass, or horns; they all ended up in our basement. John and I lived in a house for about four years, and once Dave Shogren joined us, we had the nucleus of the original Doobie Brothers.

Skip Spence, meanwhile, had met Pat Simmons. 'One night, I was at the laundromat,' Simmons writes, 'waiting while my clothes were drying. The doors swing open, and in walks Skip Spence. I was awestruck but still mustered the courage to say hello to him and tell him how great I thought he was.' Spence and Simmons were neighbours, they learned, and Spence suggested that Simmons should call around with his guitar. Simmons didn't see Spence for another year until Simmons' acoustic duo (with banjo player Peter Grant) opened a show for Spence in Campbell, a southern suburb of San Jose. Spence's backing band for the night: Pud.

'We played the north coast of California,' Simmons said later, 'and one night, we were playing a gig at the Gaslighter Theater, in Campbell. They had hired Hot Tuna and asked if we wanted to open. But when Peter and I walked in, Hot Tuna wasn't there. I asked, 'What's going on?' The owner said, 'Skip Spence, from the Moby Grape, is gonna play. He's got a band with another guy.' Well, Skip showed up as we were finishing our set, followed by John Hartman, Tom and bass player Greg Murphy. So they walk in with their amps and set them onstage. I was very curious to see what was gonna happen. Well, they started playing, and Skip started doing what he did – kind of spacing out onstage. But the other three were playing their hearts out; Tommy was playing and singing, and they did some original tunes. I was blown away. I thought, 'Wow, this guy can really sing and play.' It wasn't necessarily my type of music. I was way, way more into traditional acoustic music at that time. These guys had a much bigger sound, but I could still appreciate how talented they were.'

Johnston, in turn, was impressed with Simmons' playing: 'We were knocked out by how good they were', he said, 'Pat is an incredible fingerpicker... they were playing folk/blues type stuff and some bluegrass. We were playing rock 'n' roll. So it was an interesting evening.'

'When they finished their set,' Simmons said, 'I walked up and asked Skip, 'How're you doin'?' He said, 'Hey, Pat. Let me introduce you to the guys.' So he introduced me to Tom and John, and they said, 'We saw you playing, you guys were great.' Then Tom told me, 'You gotta come by the house. Bring your guitar, and we'll jam.' But I didn't go over. I don't know why, but I didn't. Then, one day, I was standing in my yard and up walks John. He goes, 'You gotta come by the house, man. We're trying to put a band together. It's me and Tom, and we got another bass player, and Skip's gonna play and maybe Peter Lewis [another member of Moby Grape]. We want to do some harmonies and some cool guitar interplay.' So, a few days later, I went by. There was no jam going on, but Tom and John were there, and we played some acoustic guitar at a table in the backyard. We played for hours, jamming on some of my tunes and some of his stuff. That was how we started getting to know each other, musically.'

In due course, the four-piece lineup of Tom Johnston, Pat Simmons, John Hartman and Dave Shogren came together. 'We knew we had something cool, Simmons recalled. 'Most bands might have one guy who can really sing, and one good guitar player, and everybody else was kind of excess baggage. But we had three singers – myself, Tom and the bass player at the time, Dave Shogren, whom I went to high school with. So we had three-part harmony – the John, Paul, George thing. Tom, likewise, understood that great harmony singing and great guitar playing brought something extra to a performance.'

They named themselves The Doobie Brothers in September 1970, just ahead of their debut show at the Chateau Liberté in the Santa Cruz mountains, about a 30-minute drive from downtown San Jose. (Point of trivia: the band are shown outside the club on the cover of their debut album.)'Evidently, some of the guys were sitting around the breakfast table one morning,' Simmons writes, 'sprinkling pot on their cornflakes, smokin' joints and bein' crazy. They always said, 'Let's smoke a doobie', so someone in the room says, 'Hey, why don't you just call yourselves The Doobie Brothers?' We thought it was a joke, but we were going to use it for the gig and then change it to something better. But it just kind of stuck.'

'We were just too lazy to come up with another name after we played that gig at the Chateau', Johnston recalled. 'Sometimes it's best not to overthink things.'

As the band built a steady live reputation, they refined their sound into an unusual mix of rock, blues and folk. 'We were the epitome of the hard-working, hard-livin' rock 'n' roll band', Simmons told author Mark Bego. 'We used to get plastered all the time, zonked out of our brains and pull out all the stops. Every night, we were up all night, movin', groovin' and saying, 'Let's get a beer', 'Give me a toot!' It was real fast living. We were just walking around like zombies. We were doing it for all it was worth because we figured it's gonna last a couple of years and then we're going back to where we started.'

Johnston: 'The Chateau Liberté was kind of a biker bar mixed with students, hippies and local mountain folk, and because we became popular, everybody thought of us as a 'biker band'. But we were making music for everybody. We didn't consider ourselves anything other than a band that was growing and developing.'

At Skip Spence's suggestion, they recorded several original songs at Pacific Recording in San Mateo for a demo tape. Eight of these were briefly (and illegally) released on Pickwick Records in 1980 under the title *Introducing The Doobie Brothers* and have since been bootlegged under that title and others. The recordings showcased the band's dual lead electric guitars, three-part harmonies and frenetic drumming and earned the rock group a contract at Warner Bros. Records. 'We hadn't planned on making an album at all,' Simmons told *Sounds*, 'but the demos came out so good that we decided to send them into Warner Bros. – and they liked them.'

'The moment I heard this tape by a group called The Doobie Brothers,' in-house producer Ted Templeman said, 'I knew there was something going on. I knew that I had to meet this band and see them play in person.'

'Ted took the tape into an A&R meeting,' Pat Simmons told Bob Harris of BBC Radio 2 in 2025, 'and played [the tape]. They responded positively.'

Templeman, who had been a member of Harpers Bizarre in the 1960s, joined A&R Lenny Waronker to fly to San Jose from Los Angeles to see the band perform at Chateau Liberté. 'Here's these two straight guys with penny loafers', Simmons recalled. 'Their eyes were as big as saucers. We did 'Jesus Is Just Alright', an early version of 'Long Train Runnin'' and 'Rockin' Down The Highway' – songs we would be famous for. That night, the crowd went crazy. They sat in a corner, and we knew who they were.'

'We blew the roof off the place that night', Johnston confirmed. 'I think [Templeman and Waronker] were kind of taken aback. They thought of us as more of a laid-back, semi-acoustic band, but that's not what we were. I mean, we had elements of that, but we kept it rocking pretty hard at the Chateau.'

'I loved them the moment I saw them', Templeman noted. 'They had a great look and a great sound. They were raw and definitely untested. But just a ton of potential. I wanted to work with these guys. What I didn't know was that these guys would eventually help define me as a producer just as much as I would try to define them as a band.'

The Doobie Brothers signed to Warner Bros. and started recording their debut album in November 1970. 'When we did the first album, we'd never really been together as a group at all', Pat Simmons later told *Sounds*. 'We were all old friends, and we just got high in the studios.'

Tom Johnston: 'My memories of recording the first album in San Mateo are that we all thought we were going to get a chance to continue to do what we did onstage on the record. But Lenny wanted a more acoustic and clean electric guitar style. It is true that we had songs like this written along with all the other tunes we played live, and some of them got played at gigs, but we also did a lot of high-energy, jam-style tunes that resonated with the crowds we were in front of. Both Lenny and Ted were great about giving direction and ideas for arrangements. But Ted did the largest part of the 'communicating' with us. And when we finished the album, we were all pretty excited about where we 'thought' this was all headed. We had cut our first album on a real label, and we had the single 'Nobody' picked out.'

The Doobie Brothers was released in April 1971. On the back of the album, the following appears: 'The Doobie Brothers are not the neatest new band from England, not studio musicians in search of stardom, not relatives of Warner Bros. employees, not even brothers. They are four San Jose (as distinguished from San Francisco) musicians conveniently described as a street band. That is, they share a common history of playing obscure clubs, bars and parties. They've paid their Doobie doos. This is their first album.'

Today, that album presents the Doobie Brothers in a raw, formative phase – acoustic-driven, country-rock infused and full of potential rather than polish. It's a promising but undercooked blend of biker rock and acoustic jams, but its foundational strengths – tight playing, harmony vocals and acoustic sensibility – laid crucial groundwork for the oncoming success. There are flashes of the tightness and harmonies that would later define The Doobie Brothers (and at least two great tracks, in 'Nobody' and 'Closer Each Day'), but this record is a much scrappier affair than what would follow. If you listen closely, you can already hear the hallmarks of harmony, musicianship and song craft that would define the Doobies' evolution.

Despite national advertising and an extensive tour with Mother Earth (the Mother/Brothers Tour), *The Doobie Brothers* failed to register on the album charts. Likewise, three singles taken from the album were not hits. It would take another album to refine the formula, but this is where the story begins.

'Nobody' (Johnston)

Released as a single (with B-side 'Slippery St. Paul') on 26 May 1971. Charts: did not chart

Reissued as a single (with B-side 'Flying Cloud') in 1974. Charts: US: 58

'Nobody' is the blueprint for the early sound of The Doobie Brothers, even if the song itself is a knot of paranoia and self-doubt. The chugging rhythm is provided by acoustic guitars, and 20-year-old Tom Johnston's distinctive voice is joined by spiralling harmonies in a sneakily catchy chorus. The instrumental section (2:10 to 3:04) mixes driving acoustic guitar with a loud electric guitar solo and some tricky dynamics. It suggests a band with real ensemble chemistry, honed by many gigs in and around San Jose and the Bay area.

'Nobody' was remixed for the single release, with about eight seconds snipped from the middle of the song. Although not a hit in 1971, three years later it was reissued and crept into the bottom end of the charts. The Doobie Brothers thought enough of the song to re-record it in 2010 for *World Gone Crazy* (better arranged, although the original remains the more atmospheric version) and again with Charlie Worsham for *Southbound* in 2014.

'Slippery St. Paul' (Simmons)
Country-fried acoustic guitars also underpin Pat Simmons' folksy 'Slippery St. Paul'. The humorous lyrics seem to celebrate mortality whilst strolling through a swamp. The arrangement and approach are certainly more rustic than the band's later sound, closer to a jug band than anything else, complete with communal vocals, banjo and honky-tonk piano. There's charm in its looseness, but one senses the band are still trying on hats rather than wearing one of their own. The song is a sideways swipe at Paul Curcio, owner of Pacific Recording Studios. Curcio later established Music America Studios, where he produced Metallica's debut, *Kill 'Em All*. The later 'Little Martha' (The Allman Brothers Band) and 'Penny For Your Thoughts' (Peter Frampton) share a clear DNA with 'Slippery St. Paul', especially its closing moments.

'Greenwood Creek' (Johnston)
This country blues is tightly arranged, with an attractive groove. The ensemble playing is appealing, and we have a rare harmonica solo by Tom Johnston. The song ambles along amiably, with a whiff of *Workingman's Dead*-era Grateful Dead in its acoustic strumming and country-tinged melody. The harmonies are tentative but present. It's not a standout track, but it offers a welcome change of pace and shows early signs of the band's versatility.

'It Won't Be Right' (Johnston, Simmons)
The short, punchy 'It Won't Be Right' blends funk rhythms with fast-strummed guitar. It showcases early experimentation with groove, a sharp, Motown-inflected vamp with tight acoustic guitar stabs and a strong vocal from Tom Johnston. Lyrically, it's standard early-1970s relationship fare, but there's a confidence in the performance that belies the band's inexperience. One can certainly hear the seeds of 'Long Train Runnin'' in the rhythm guitar. It's short and to the point. Blink and you'll miss it, but not without nodding your head.

'Travelin' Man' (Johnston)

The gentle 'Travelin' Man' reminds the listener of the work of The Eagles and fellow Warners artists America, neither of whom had recorded their debut albums yet. All three bands shared the same influences of American roots music and bright harmonies. It's interesting to speculate how The Doobies' career might have developed by focusing on this reflective style, which is a long way from the exuberance of their live act at the time.

Tom Johnston's lead vocal is more relaxed here, and the chorus is oddly affecting. The lyrics paint the singer as a weary wanderer – a trope that would return throughout the Doobies' career. There's a subtle shift in dynamics around the instrumental break that hints at the more polished arrangements to come. 'Travelin' Man' is not essential, but it is indicative of a band learning how to structure a song.

'Feelin' Down Farther' (Johnston)

Released as a single (with B-side 'Travelin' Man') in September 1971. Charts: did not chart

'Feelin' Down Farther' has a slight touch of psychedelia, with moody vocals, an unusual intensity and a bit of wah-wah guitar buried in the mix, which gives it a slight funk edge. Variants of the familiar guitar riff and vocal melodies of the following year's 'Listen To The Music' make their debut here, but without the exuberating commerciality of the latter song's uplifting chorus.

'The Master' (Johnston)

'The Master' sounds so much like 'Feelin' Down Farther' that if you're not paying attention, then you might be forgiven for thinking that you'd skipped back to the previous track on the album. At times, it threatens to morph into a cover of Van Morrison's 'Caravan', but there are pleasing flashes of electric jazz and some delightful bluegrass electric guitar playing in the central section. They don't quite pull it off on this song, but the intent is impressive.

'Growin' A Little Each Day' (Johnston)

Tom Johnston plays piano on this melodic and somewhat introspective song. The harmonies and emotional delivery provide early evidence of the band's songwriting depth. There's a delicate melodic sensibility here, even if the playing is hesitant.

'The Beehive State' (Newman)

Released as a single (with B-side 'Closer Each Day') in November 1971. Charts: did not chart

'Beehive State' is a loud, quirky, live-in-the-studio cover of a Randy Newman song from his debut album, released in 1968. It's a novelty song about Utah, played with tongue firmly in cheek and replacing Newman's weary ragtime with a brutal twin-guitar attack. The main riff has a strong echo of 'Life In The Fast Lane' and the song as a whole gives us some idea of how The Doobie Brothers might have sounded at the Chateau Liberté. Musically, it's tight, even funky, but the lyrics border on absurdist satire. It doesn't fit at all, but that's part of its charm. The band are searching for *something* here, but haven't yet found it.

'Closer Every Day' (Simmons)
Pat Simmons' 'Closer Every Day' is a highlight of the debut album. It starts slowly, with a subtle intensity and impressive vocal interplay. Two minutes in, the song kicks into a higher gear with a rolling groove, loud, locked-in rhythm guitars and a bright guitar solo. 'Closer Every Day' bridges the band's early folk-rock style to the more groove-oriented songs to come on their next album. Here is The Doobies' first-era blueprint in miniature.

'Chicago' (arr. Simmons)
The album closes with a delightful mix of acoustic blues and bluegrass. It seemingly blends Robert Johnson's 'Sweet Home Chicago' with Jimmy Reed's 'Bright Lights, Big City'; a simple end to an earthy, understated record, as though The Doobies are playing on your back porch.

Toulouse Street (1972)

Personnel:
Tom Johnston: vocals, guitars
Patrick Simmons: vocals, guitars, banjo, recorder
Tiran Porter: backing vocals, bass
John Hartman: drums, percussion
Michael Hossack: drums, steel drums
With:
Dave Shogren: bass, acoustic guitar, backing vocals
Bill Payne: piano, organ
Jerry Jumonville, Jon Robert Smith and Joe Lane Davis: saxophones
Sherman Marshall Cyr: trumpet
Ted Templeman: percussion
Recorded at Pacific, San Mateo, California, between 1971 and 1972
Produced by Ted Templeman
Released: July 1972
Highest chart positions. US: 21. UK: did not chart

The Doobie Brothers' sophomore album presents a much stronger set of songs, paired with a muscular new rhythm section of bassist Tiran Porter, originally from Los Angeles, and second drummer Michael Hossack. Initial recording sessions in July and between September and October 1971 by the original four-piece were self-produced. These were rejected by Warner Bros. '*Toulouse Street* was made over two time periods', Tom Johnston said in 2024. 'The first sessions weren't that good because we hadn't started working with Ted Templeman yet. We had started recording songs up in San Francisco at Wally Heider's, and we didn't come up with anything that was really catchy. Warner Bros., our label, let us know that.'

Several songs from these sessions were later made available on the *Long Train Running* box set in 1999. Shogren left at this point, to be replaced by Tiran Porter, who had been in a folk trio, Scratch, with Pat Simmons and a violinist called Mike Mindel. Porter was a formidable musician and an excellent singer. He would spend just over nine years with the band. Johnston: 'Sometimes you just find the perfect guy at the perfect time. That was Tiran.'

Michael Hossack sat in when his band Morning Reign played the same venue as The Doobies. Some sources say that this was at Bimbo's 365 Club in San Francisco; Pat Simmons remembers this taking place at Chateau Liberté. Either way, the outcome was the same. 'Mike had his drums sitting up on stage', Simmons said, 'John Hartman asked, 'Do you mind if Mike sits in with us?' Mike started playing [with us], and we went, 'Oh, my god, what a fabulous drummer…' And then, I dunno, about a week later, John Hartman asked us about having two drummers. And we said, 'Really, John, do you think you want to do that?' And he said, 'Yes, it would be really cool, we'd be like The Allman Brothers.' We agreed to try it, and that was the five-piece for *Toulouse Street*.'

Under the production guidance of Ted Templeman (a name that will become as synonymous with the Doobies as George Martin is with The Beatles), The Doobie Brothers' new lineup alchemised a rare and potent combination of tight songwriting, muscular playing and Californian sheen. *Toulouse Street* has the energy and depth of a debut album and delivers a rich blend of country, bluegrass, folk, blues and rootsy rock. The Doobie Brothers' signature sound – at least in their first phase – starts here. It's not just a genuine statement of intent but also an album of beginnings – of voices finding harmony, guitars finding swagger and a band finding direction. While not as cohesive or sonically rich as the later *The Captain And Me*, it has a freshness and variety that remains endearing. Few albums blend biker-rock, folk, gospel and funk quite so naturally. It is here, on *Toulouse Street*, that The Doobie Brothers find their identity. Ironically, as it turns out, they needed to understand that they were never just one thing: *Toulouse Street* is the sound of them becoming several and embracing all of them.

'And those days, you could have a whole album that stiffed – which we did.' Tom Johnston told *Songfacts*. 'But the label believed in the band, and they believed that we would eventually come up with something that would happen and stuck behind us, gave us some money to make the records. And consequently, it all paid off.'

The lead single, 'Listen To The Music', offers a sunny mix of funk and folk and helped push *Toulouse Street* to number 21 on the *Billboard* album charts.

In a significant change to the band's sound palette, Little Feat's Bill Payne would add his distinctive musicianship to this album and several more in the future, as well as joining the band as an adjunct member for live dates between 2015 and 2021.

From September 1972, The Doobie Brothers promoted *Toulouse Street* with a tour supporting British glam-rockers T. Rex, led by Marc Bolan. 'Watching him and his band every night was influential, I think, for all of us in The Doobie Brothers', Pat Simmons reflected. 'He was taking things to another level when it came to production, costumes and everything else. It was a real education. I think what we learned watching him was that if you really wanted to endear yourself to an audience, then you had to be a little bigger than life. You had to dress the part, and you had to act the part. Watching him, I started thinking to myself, 'Wow, I need to change the way I dress. I needed to have a more rock 'n' roll attitude.' And I think everybody in our band was thinking along similar lines.'

As the year progressed, the band would also play shows with the likes of Edgar Winter, Loggins and Messina, Montrose, Rare Earth, Bob Seger, Jim Croce, Chicago and Billy Preston.

'Listen To The Music' (Johnston)

Released as a single (with B-side 'Toulouse Street') on 19 July 1972. Charts: US: 11, UK: 29

Featured on Best Of The Doobies (1976)

'Listen To The Music' was the big bang. It transformed The Doobie Brothers into a household name. It introduced them to American radio and kept them there for the next ten years.

'This one came about in my bedroom in San Jose – early 1972 or maybe late 1971', Tom Johnston told *Guitar Player* in 2024. 'That's actually one of the few songs I just sat down and wrote and had everything, words and music, at the same time. I came up with a lick and started putting the words together, and called Ted [Templeman]. Woke him up at two in the morning, or something like that, which he wasn't really happy about. I played it for him over the phone, and he said, 'Yeah, maybe. Call me tomorrow.' So I did, and he said, 'Let's get it down here and see what we can do with it in the studio.' I thought it was a single; it's the only time in my life I've ever had that feeling. We hadn't had one yet – at least not one that was successful, I should say. So we got down in the studio, and we kept it pretty much the same as it was. The lyrics all stayed the same; the chords all stayed the same.'

The upbeat, sunshiny arrangement mixes a simple but catchy guitar strum and an infectious chorus. Tom Johnston's lyrics underpin a peace-and-love anthem that stops just shy of being naïve. 'I thought people would get along a lot better if they used music to communicate rather than political rhetoric', Johnston said. 'I was trying to give it a utopian view, I guess. The idea was that music could lift humans up – including world leaders, if they were able to sit down on some big grassy hill where the sun was shining and listen to music. Then they would figure out that everybody had more in common than they thought and that no disagreement was worth getting so bent out of shape about. So the world could benefit from the point of view that music could make everything better.'

The lyrics are elevated by the sheer joy of the arrangement: listen again to the rolling piano (courtesy of Bill Payne), the bouncing bass, the flanging on the chorus, Pat Simmons' vocal solo spot in the bridge ('Like a lazy flowing river/Surrounding castles in the sky') and the gospel-tinged backing vocals, especially in the last few repeats of the chorus. There is also a banjo. 'We were working on the song,' noted Pat Simmons, 'and I thought, 'What if we had banjo here?' I knew it was off the wall, and I'm not really a great banjo player, but I wondered what it would sound like. Ted looked at me sideways when I said it! He said, 'What? Nobody plays banjo on rock 'n' roll records!' But he was always cool about letting us try stuff, even if we didn't use it. So I gave it a try, and afterwards, he said, 'Man, that's so cool.' So we kept banjo on the chorus.'

Banjo or not, by 1972 standards, 'Listen To The Music' is polished West Coast pop with a boogie core. It still holds up remarkably well. 'I remember first hearing it in my Volkswagen', Tom Johnston told *Vintage Guitar* years later. 'We were pretty much living on food stamps and brown rice, paying 40 bucks a month rent and playing as many gigs as we could. But when that song hit, we started getting a little bit more money for gigs, started playing organised shows and started becoming a professional unit.'

The single version is remixed, running a few bpm faster and with a much quicker fade – it's over a minute shorter than the album cut. Put this song on a playlist with America's 'Ventura Highway', Seals & Crofts' 'Summer Breeze', Loggins & Messina's 'Danny's Song' and James Taylor's 'Your Smiling Face'.

'Rockin' Down The Highway' (Johnston)

Featured on Best Of The Doobies (1976)

This is straight-up, urgent rock 'n' roll, one of the band's most popular songs over the years. 'Rockin' Down The Highway' is a high-energy track with chugging guitars and lyrics celebrating freedom on the road. Bill Payne's piano playing, mixed high on the left channel, is a key element. 'Rockin' Down The Highway' effortlessly captures the ethos of the open road. "Rockin' Down the Highway' is about being on Highway 17, going between San Jose and Santa Cruz, and being up in the Santa Cruz mountains', Tom Johnston said. 'It's basically about having the top down and having a ball, being footloose and fancy free in that era. This was one of my early songs. I'd written the chorus probably before the band were even together… I just liked the chord change and built around that, combined the bridge and, like a lot of songs, found other chords to enhance so it's not just a straight I-IV-V. It mostly wrote itself, including the words, which is always the most fun. I developed the rest of the song after that with the Doobies in the studio while we were making *Toulouse Street*. It's not hard to figure out why 'Rockin' Down The Highway' caught on as it did. People loved that song, and it still goes over really well.'

The timing and phrasing of the vocals in the chorus are perhaps too close to 'Listen To The Music', but the song is a showcase for Tom Johnston's love of rhythm-driven rock. A few years later, Bachman-Turner Overdrive would write their own ode to the road, 'Roll On Down The Highway'.

'Rockin' Down the Highway' was remixed when it was released as the B-side of 'Listen To The Music' in July 1972.

'Mamaloi' (Simmons)

Patrick Simmons takes the reins for this surprising shift in tone: a gentle, reggae-inflected track. 'Mamaloi' is an early indicator of how, across The Doobies' career, Simmons' eclecticism offered a welcome contrast to Johnston's intensity (and, later, to Michael McDonald's romanticism). 'Mamaloi' is brief, breezy and lightly exotic. Its placement as track three is canny as it relaxes the listener after the opening one-two punch of high-octane rock. It lets the album exhale. There's a charm in its economy – nothing is overstated, nothing drags.

'Toulouse Street' (Simmons)
Pat Simmons wrote the bluesy, dark, moody and soulful 'Toulouse Street' when on tour promoting the band's debut album, *The Doobie Brothers*. 'We hit New Orleans', Simmons told Mark Bego. 'At the time, I really wasn't sure where we were going, or if we were going anywhere. That's when I wrote 'Toulouse Street'. When I wrote the refrain – 'I just might pass this way again' – I really wasn't sure that I ever would.'

It's the most atmospheric piece on the album. The woodwind arrangement is tastefully minimal and adds a cinematic texture. The harmonies are ghostly rather than gleaming. Simmons delivers an emotional, closely-mic'd vocal over a slow, winding acoustic groove. 'Toulouse Street' adds a twist of noir to an otherwise sun-drenched album.

'Cotton Mouth' (Seals, Crofts)
'Cotton Mouth' was originally written and recorded by Seals & Crofts (the 'Summer Breeze' guys). It's a curious but enjoyable inclusion. The Doobies beef up the song significantly, transforming it from gentle folk-pop into a crunchy, percussive, horn-laden funk number. Tom Johnston takes the lead vocals and sounds fully at home here, delivering the verses with a bluesy snarl. There are touches of gospel and New Orleans blues in the arrangement, which place the song with peers such as Dr. John's 'Such A Night', Van Morrison's 'Domino' and The Band's 'Life Is A Carnival'. The horns – an uncommon texture for The Doobie Brothers at this stage – point ahead to the more soul-inflected work they'd do with Michael McDonald later in the decade.

'Don't Start Me To Talkin'' (Williamson)
This is a straightforward, raw and energetic cover of a Sonny Boy Williamson blues classic, loose and playful with a live jam feel reminiscent of the harmony guitars of The Allman Brothers Band. Bill Payne trills on piano, and the horns cook up a storm. As ever with blues numbers, the trick is to play it like you mean it – and the Doobies just about get away with it, with a barroom vocal delivery and two loud guitar solos. It's not too hard to imagine them singing this in the Château Liberté in their early days. That said, it adds little to the original, and they very quickly moved away from this style of music after this album.

'Jesus Is Just Alright' (Reynolds)
Released as a single (with B-side 'Rockin' Down The Highway') on 15 November 1972. Charts: US: 35
Featured on Best Of The Doobies (1976)
'Jesus Is Just Alright' was written by Art Reynolds and first recorded by Reynolds' group, The Art Reynolds Singers, for their 1966 album, *Tellin' It Like It Is*. This is upbeat gospel, with a tight piano/bass/drums rhythm combo and

echoing choral vocals. The song was reconstructed into a rock arrangement by The Byrds on their album *Ballad Of Easy Rider* (1969) and was soon a staple of bar and college bands. The Doobies' version leans on The Byrds', but is faster, funkier and vastly more muscular. Johnston and Simmons trade vocal duties, and the arrangement builds steadily into a multi-voice call-and-response workout. The powerful instrumental dynamics include a mid-song breakdown and build-up, which is classic Doobies.

'White Sun' (Johnston)
In a complete change of mood, this acoustic-led tune has philosophical lyrics and provides a more introspective, mystical mood. Harmonies are soft and layered, pastoral and poetic. It feels at times like something Crosby, Stills & Nash might have attempted if they'd grown up riding motorcycles in San Jose. There's a sense of yearning here, both musically and lyrically, and it's one of Tom Johnston's earliest glimpses of his rare folkier side. A quiet highlight.

'Disciple' (Johnston)
At nearly seven minutes, 'Disciple' is the album's epic, freewheeling and expansive country rocker with distorted electric guitars and high-octane jam-band energy. The vocal and musical interplay between Johnston and Simmons is especially strong here – an early indication of their chemistry as dual front men. The song doesn't so much end as accelerate into chaos. Ted Templeman's production, which has a very live feel and keeps overdubs to a minimum, reins things in just enough to keep it on track. In concert, this would become a platform for extended solos and jamming.

'Snake Man' (Johnston)
Clocking in at under two minutes, 'Snake Man' is an acoustic blues which feels like a half-finished sketch – dirty, raw and just a touch sinister. Johnston's vocal is snarled rather than sung, and the guitar tone is all dust and grime. It ends the album not with resolution, but with attitude – a sideways grin instead of a handshake.

The Captain And Me (1973)

Personnel:
Tom Johnston: vocals, guitars, synthesiser, harmonica
Patrick Simmons: vocals, guitars, ARP synthesiser, banjo
Tiran Porter: backing vocals, bass
John Hartman: backing vocals, drums, percussion
Michael Hossack: drums, congas, timbales
With:
Bill Payne: piano, organ, electric piano
Jeffrey 'Skunk' Baxter: pedal steel guitar
Ted Templeman: percussion, backing vocals
Recorded at Warner Bros. Studios, North Hollywood, California, between 1972 and 1973
Produced by Ted Templeman
Released: 2 March 1973.
Highest chart positions. US: 7, UK: did not chart

The Captain And Me, their first top ten album, established The Doobie Brothers in the front rank of American rock music. It perfectly captures the band in that brief, golden moment when laid-back West Coast boogie met clever studio craft. As with many albums of the early 1970s, it's an artefact of contrasts: communal yet precise, warm yet punchy, effortlessly commercial but not without musical guile. *The Captain And Me* nimbly straddles the two central tensions of the early-period Doobie Brothers: Tom Johnston's chugging, radio-friendly riff-rock and Pat Simmons' more contemplative folk-blues sensibility. That these coexist without ever feeling at odds is part of the band's alchemy: it's only later, when Michael McDonald joins the band, that two different styles start to move apart, and it was Simmons who needed to change to fit in.

An important guest musician adds some spice: Steely Dan's Jeff 'Skunk' Baxter. A former member of the psychedelic rock band Ultimate Spinach, he later played with the Holy Modal Rounders in New York before moving to Los Angeles as a session guitarist. In August 1972, he became a founding member of Steely Dan and recorded his contributions to *The Captain And Me* between his recording and performance commitments to Steely Dan. Steely Dan and The Doobie Brothers would play several shows together in both 1973 and 1974 (the latter included a young backing singer called Michael McDonald), and Baxter would join them on stage occasionally. The Doobies would also play shows in this period with Steve Miller, Dr Hook And The Medicine Show, Frank Zappa, Rare Earth, Mike Bloomfield, Chicago, the Beach Boys, Loggins And Messina, Jim Croce, Foghat, It's A Beautiful Day, Hot Tuna and Quicksilver Messenger Service.

'Natural Thing' (Johnston)

The Captain And Me opens, appropriately enough, with a riff, although this one is gentle and less aggressive than other early Johnston compositions. This sets the tone for the rest of the album – mid-tempo and unmistakably Californian but with a touch of grit. Tom Johnston's voice, gravelly and impassioned, is at the fore here, singing elliptical, slightly nonsensical lyrics ('I'm gonna change my method/Get me a big ham bone/Gonna make all the leaders of the country/Get it together and bring it on home'). It's the groove and the bright chorus that do the heavy lifting, re-establishing some familiar Doobies tropes with a new precision.

A subtle use of soft synthesisers gives the song a deceptive richness. Tom and Pat had heard Stevie Wonder's *Talking Book* and met the gifted musician whilst on tour in the UK. The use of synthesisers on 'Natural Thing' comes directly from this meeting, and they employed Malcolm Cecil and Robert Margouleff from the pioneering duo Tonto's Expanding Head Band to assist. 'They brought out this giant cabinet with quarter-inch plugs and banks of oscillators', Simmons recalled. 'Each oscillator had a different waveform. There was a rolling waveform and a spike waveform – these guys would combine them and then control the sound with a keyboard. They could get just one note at a time. It was really slow and really tedious, but totally worth it once you heard what they were doing.'

'I think Malcolm and Robert were characters in their own right', Johnston agreed. 'I think having them in the studio added a cool atmosphere. Not a lot of American bands were experimenting like this. I'm not sure we ever got much credit for it. 'Natural Thing' was a departure from any style we'd recorded before.'

'Long Train Runnin'' (Johnston)

Released as a single (with B-side: 'Without You') in March 1973. Charts: US: 8. UK: 7
Featured on Best Of The Doobies (1976)

Here is The Doobie Brothers' first top ten single, the engine room of their commercial ascent. Interestingly, this began life as a throwaway jam called 'Osborne'. 'We played [it] every night even though we hadn't written words to it', Tom Johnston noted in 2011. 'I'd make them up every night, and the song would take on the names of 'Rosey Pig Mosley' or 'Parliament' or whatever the heck else!'

The song might never have been properly recorded had producer Templeman not spotted its potential. 'Ted requested that we record it for *The Captain And Me*. I told him, 'It doesn't have any words. I just make 'em up every night.' And he said, 'Well ... Write some, man!' I said, 'Yeah, good point. But are you sure you want me to do this? 'Cause it's really just a jam.' And he said, 'I think it could be great. Why don't you write it about a train or something?' So I walked into another room at Amigo Studios – we were constantly working there for about four or five years – and I wrote the words for it, brought 'em back and put 'em down. The song came to fruition like that. To my surprise, it ended up being a popular song. I really didn't expect much out of it.'

The rhythmic strumming that opens the song is pure Johnston – percussive and propulsive. The catchy hook ('without love'), popping congas and harmonica solo make the song ideal for FM radio. The lyrics are impressionistic at best, but who cares when the rhythm section swings like this?

'China Grove' (Johnston)

Released as a single (with B-side 'Evil Woman') in July 1973. Charts: US: 15
Featured on Best Of The Doobies (1976)

'China Grove' has been the cornerstone of The Doobie Brothers' back catalogue for over 50 years. 'This is one I wrote in the bedroom in San Jose', explained the song's composer, Tom Johnston. 'I just started playing that main lick on the acoustic guitar and thought, 'This would be great on electric!' I don't know if I was thinking in a 'hit' vein at that point or not.'

'China Grove' opens with a loud series of power chords (E, D, C#m, A, E). '['China Grove' was] only a heavier version of what we had done up to that point', Johnston wrote. John Hartman and Michael Hossack developed an aggressive, driving backbeat (in the final mix, each drummer is panned hard left and right, as are the guitars, with vocals and bass in the centre).

The mythos of the song – a fictionalised Texan town full of samurai and students – is Johnston again letting imagery take precedence over meaning. 'Billy Payne came up with the Chinese-sounding piano part in the bridge', Johnston recalled [listen at 1:51]. 'That sparked my idea for the lyrics, and so I ran with it.'

When the sun comes up on a sleepy little town
Down around San Antone
And the folks are risin' for another day
Roundabout their homes

Subconsciously, Johnston name-checks an actual town called China Grove, which is situated on the eastern edge of San Antonio, Texas.

Listen to how the band lock into each other's playing; every note feels necessary, with a tightness to the groove that parallels the work of Little Feat. The rolling piano stabs are courtesy of Bill Payne's outstanding contribution. 'China Grove' is so infectious that it's no surprise the song quickly became a staple of The Doobies' live shows.

The song, according to bassist Tiran Porter, confused the music press. 'We have been overlooked by the press', he said. 'After the first LP, the only people who seemed to accept us were beer-crazed bikers. By the time our second album, *Toulouse Street*, was released, we got a lot of attention because of the single ['Listen To The Music'], but we were dismissed as hippie hard-rockers. Then we hit in 1973 with a couple of singles ['Long Train Runnin'' and 'China Grove'] and critics called us top 40 rock bubblegum.'

Thankfully, their listeners responded well to the genre-blending of the early-period Doobies. *The Captain And Me* is seen as one of their most polished and successful early albums, showcasing the twin guitars, dual drummers, rich vocal harmonies and a genre fluidity that would come to define their sound.

It was no accident that 'China Grove' was placed as the first track on the massively selling *Best Of The Doobies* album in 1976.

'Dark Eyed Cajun Woman' (Johnston)

Tom Johnston's work throughout his time with The Doobie Brothers sometimes brought a moodier, bluesier palette. 'Dark-Eyed Cajun Woman' is a slow burner with strong echoes of BB King in its stately pace. 'It's kind of a tribute to BB King', Johnston admitted in an interview with Bob Harris in 2025. 'He had a huge influence on me.'

The guitar solo is particularly lyrical, underpinned by a swooning string section which harks back to King's arrangement of 'The Thrill Is Gone' (1969). 'The hair was standing up on the back of my neck when we got to do that track', Johnston said. 'That was a big deal.'

Lyrically, it's the age-old trope of the mysterious, unattainable woman – half homage, half cliché – but the sonic atmosphere redeems it. It's a change of pace that works beautifully at this point in the album's running order.

'Clear As The Driven Snow' (Simmons)

Here is the Doobie Brothers at their most openly experimental. 'Clear As The Driven Snow' begins with a delicate acoustic introduction, its lilting, almost medieval feel setting a mood that is both pastoral and reflective. Pat Simmons, often the band's folkier conscience, leads the way with a vocal that is understated yet quietly persuasive. The lyric is as opaque as many of his contributions – evocative but elusive, more concerned with impression than clarity.

The song is a study in contrasts. For four minutes, it drifts along gently, introspective and spacious, allowing the acoustic textures to breathe. Then, almost without warning, the track transforms into a cascading electric jam. Guitars take over, percussion grows busier and the reflective tone of the opening is swept aside in a storm of rhythm and melody. The shift is dramatic but not jarring: it feels earned, as if the first half was preparing the listener for the sudden surge of energy.

Simmons was never the flashiest member of the band, but this piece demonstrates his ambition. It was unusual for the Doobies to stretch out in this way, and the result stands out within their catalogue. It is not difficult to imagine the same material interpreted by Crosby, Stills, Nash & Young, by America, or given extended improvisational treatment by the Grateful Dead. The Doobies may not have pursued that road often, but with 'Clear As The Driven Snow', they proved they were capable of broadening their palette.

'Without You' (Hartman, Hossack, Johnston, Porter, Simmons)
Featured on Best Of The Doobies (1976)
A rare full-band composition, 'Without You' is among the heaviest tracks in the Doobies' early catalogue. Dense with guitar overdubs and propelled by chugging riffs, it leans directly on the influence of The Who. Multi-tracked vocals add to the weight, creating a wall of sound that pushes the band squarely into early arena-rock territory.

John Hartman and Michael Hossack deserve special mention here. With two drummers panned far left and right, the stereo effect is powerful, giving the track a rhythmic muscle that was uncommon for the period. Their powerhouse playing makes the song a live favourite, and in concert, it often became a climactic set-closer, complete with smoke, explosions and maximum volume.

Melodically, it is not the most memorable item in their catalogue, but that is not the point. Its function is to overwhelm, to show the Doobies could match their peers in terms of sheer sonic force. It works particularly well as the final track on side two of *Best Of The Doobies* (1976), where it serves as a thunderous bookend to the compilation.

Its title, borrowed from Badfinger's 1972 number one hit, is coincidental but curious. Both songs share a similar emotional message – 'Baby, baby, I can't live without you' – yet the execution could not be more different. Where Badfinger offered melodic melancholy, the Doobies delivered volume, density and impact.

'South City Midnight Lady' (Simmons)
Featured on Best Of The Doobies (1976)
'South City Midnight Lady' stands in stark contrast to the heaviness of 'Without You'. This is Pat Simmons' masterpiece on the album, a song of rare beauty and genuine tenderness. The arrangement is graceful and spacious. Jeff Baxter's pedal steel guitar lends the track a country-rock edge, giving it a plaintive timbre that recalls Moby Grape at their most reflective, while the shimmering vocal harmonies echo the early Eagles. Simmons' lead vocal is unusually tender, suffused with emotion and directness not always present in his work. Unlike many of his more impressionistic lyrics, this one is a clear-eyed love song, straightforward in its emotional intent. The effect is spellbinding. The Doobies were not often associated with vulnerability, but here they achieved it without slipping into sentimentality. The song's inclusion on *Best Of The Doobies* (1976) is entirely justified, and for many listeners, it remains one of the band's most enduring ballads. Its emotional clarity, combined with the elegance of its arrangement, makes it a gem of the catalogue. Even at 5:29, this feels too short.

'Evil Woman' (Simmons)
By contrast, 'Evil Woman' is one of the weaker tracks on the album. Built around a riff-driven blues-rock pattern, it feels workmanlike, as though

constructed from familiar parts rather than inspired invention. Simmons sings with commitment, and the band play with their usual tightness, but the end result lacks freshness.

The lyric, reflecting the casual sexism of the era, has not aged well, and the music itself borrows heavily from Blind Faith's 'Had To Cry Today', with guitar lines that echo that song's phrasing a little too closely. The instrumental interplay is solid – this was, after all, a group of seasoned musicians – but the track lacks the nuance and imagination of the band's stronger material.

It is telling that 'Evil Woman' has seldom appeared in live sets. In a catalogue brimming with more inspired choices, this one quickly faded from view. It serves as a reminder that even on their strongest albums, the Doobies were not immune to the occasional lapse into formula.

'Busted Down Around O'Connelly Corners' (Luft)

This miniature acoustic interlude, written by Pat Simmons' friend Patrick Luft, lasts less than a minute. It is the first of Simmons' mood pieces – short, atmospheric fragments that would recur throughout the band's catalogue. Though slight, it has its charms. The guitar figure is simple, almost as though Simmons is sitting picking on his back porch. Its brevity is part of the appeal. In an era when many rock acts were stretching songs to epic proportions, there is something refreshing about a vignette that says its piece and then disappears. It may be a throwaway, but it adds colour and texture to the album, a gentle palate cleanser before the next full composition.

'Ukiah' (Johnston)

One of the overlooked tracks on the album, 'Ukiah' is a joyous slice of country-funk that opens with an upbeat strum and immediately settles into a breezy shuffle. The title refers to a Northern Californian town where Tom Johnston would hang out as a student. There's a distinct warmth in tone. The harmonies are especially well-crafted here, with just a hint of gospel in the backing vocals. Johnston's lyrics, though characteristically elliptical, seem more grounded than usual. The walking bass line is infectious, and the guitar solo is clean and lyrical. With its West Coast shimmer, acoustic guitars, easy swing and California breeziness, 'Ukiah' could have come from *American Beauty*-era Grateful Dead. It has that laid-back campfire mood that slides in right next to 'Sugar Magnolia' or 'Friend Of The Devil'.

'Ukiah' segues directly into the final track, functioning almost as an overture to 'The Captain And Me'. As transitions go, it's a masterstroke of album sequencing.

'The Captain And Me' (Johnston)

Part folk ballad, part electric chant, the closing 'The Captain And Me' moves through a journey, growing gradually more forceful before receding into near silence. Lyrically, it's one part nautical, two parts philosophical, but the arrangement gives it real emotional heft. The calm, pastoral soundscape features banjo, acoustic guitars, group harmony vocals, congas and timbales. The arrangement, Johnston explained, featured 'picking parts at the front, which were like Crosby, Stills & Nash; semi-rock parts… with harmony parts we all sang; and at the end, a driving rhythm, strumming and percussion behind some cool harmony lines.' The last two minutes pick up the pace, and the closing has a kind of cosmic psychedelia that reminds the listener of America's 'Ventura Highway'.

Lyrically, Tom Johnston has admitted 'the captain' has no specific meaning – the lyrics have a positive, cosmic feel, celebrating unity and collective spirit. The song's steady focus on moving forward suggests that the road (and life) is easier when people lean on one another, reinforcing the idea that companionship steadies the journey. It's a simple, clear piece of writing whose calm sense of unity gives it more weight than its plain language might first suggest.

This song typifies the band's knack for blending diverse genres. The folky, harmonically-rich arrangement contrasts markedly with the funk and boogie-infused singles 'Long Train Runnin'' and 'China Grove'. 'The Captain And Me' serves as a reflective, harmonious bookend to an otherwise energetic, groove-laden album. Structurally, it's a serene conclusion that beautifully encapsulates the band's country-folk sensibilities. Within The Doobie Brothers' catalogue, it stands as a testament to their early genre-melding artistry and the chemistry between Johnston's rock drive and Simmons' folk-tinged introspection.

What Were Once Vices Are Now Habits (1974)

Personnel:
Tom Johnston: vocals, guitars
Patrick Simmons: vocals, guitars
Tiran Porter: backing vocals, bass
John Hartman: drums, percussion
Michael Hossack: drums
Keith Knudsen: drums, backing vocals
With:
Jeff 'Skunk' Baxter: pedal steel guitar
Bill Payne: organ, piano, clavinet
James Booker: piano
Arlo Guthrie: autoharp
Eddie Guzman: percussion
Milt Holland: percussion
Wayne Jackson: trumpet
Andrew Love and James Mitchell: saxophones
Jack Hale: trombone
Novi Novog: viola
Ted Templeman: percussion
Recorded at Warner Bros, North Hollywood; Wally Heider, San Francisco; and Burbank Studios, California, in 1973
Produced by Ted Templeman
Released: 1 February 1974
Highest chart positions. US: 4, UK: 19

Michael Hossack left The Doobie Brothers in September 1973 during the recording of the band's fourth album, *What Were Once Vices Are Now Habits*. He was replaced by Keith Knudsen, who had met the band before they signed to Warner Brothers. Knudsen had been in the house band at the famed Matrix club and recorded with Blind Joe Mendlebaum Blues Band, the organist and singer Lee Michaels (appearing on three of his albums) and Hoodoo Rhythm Devils. Knudsen was playing with the band Bonaroo when he moved across to The Doobie Brothers: both bands shared the same manager. Hossack went in the opposite direction to fill the drum seat in Bonaroo. 'I knew [Knudsen] from living in Marin and hanging about with him and some other musicians in San Anselmo', Tom Johnston wrote. 'So he fit right in.' Knudsen stayed with The Doobie Brothers until the farewell tour in 1982, was instrumental in the band getting back together in 1987 and rejoined for another 12 years from 1993 to 2005. He contributed to eight of the band's studio albums in total.

With *What Were Once Vices Are Now Habits*, The Doobie Brothers found themselves at a decision point. Riding high on the success of *The Captain And Me*, they could have played it safe. Instead, they built out their sound with strings, horns, acoustic textures and a more layered studio aesthetic instead of just the tight, road-tested band vibe. There were more overdubs with guitars stacked on guitars and percussion tucked under the beat, fuller vocal arrangements evidencing time spent shaping the vocals instead of just capturing what they did live, and cleaner, more sculpted mixes. The result is an album that's adventurous and uneven in equal measure. It's also the last to feel like an organic product of the band's pre-McDonald era – a snapshot of a group still straddling biker rock, bar-band funk and sunny California gospel before drifting into smoother waters.

The overhead cover shot of the band in concert was taken on 4 December 1973 at Western Kentucky University in Bowling Green, midway between Louisville and Nashville. As their appeal spread internationally (this was their first chart album in the UK), The Doobie Brothers visited Europe in early 1974, performing four dates in the UK as well as shows in the Netherlands, Germany and Belgium.

'Song To See You Through' (Johnston)

The album opens not with the expected roar of guitars or a swaggering riff, but with something altogether more meditative: a mantra-like statement of intent. 'We're here for you,' it seems to say, 'and the music is the way we show it.'

'Song To See You Through' establishes at once that this band are broadening their horizons. Gospel inflections dominate, with Hammond organ swelling behind layered harmonies that feel unusually sincere for a group so often associated with drive and propulsion. Horns stab tastefully, never dominating but adding a sheen reminiscent of Memphis soul, while the percussion – particularly the congas – adds a warmth and swing that feels more Earth, Wind & Fire than Allman Brothers.

There is, indeed, something very post-Woodstock about this piece: a sense of communal affirmation, of deliberately wearing vulnerability on one's sleeve at a time when irony was beginning to creep into rock. It is unhip almost to the point of bravery, but that earnestness is its strength. 'Song to See You Through' doesn't rock, in the conventional Doobies sense, but it radiates a gentle luminosity. As an opener, it signals that the band are not content to remain locked into a single groove; they are seeking transcendence, even if fleetingly.

'Spirit' (Johnston)

Tom Johnston reins in his trademark bluster here in favour of something more reflective. Built around fast-picked acoustic guitar patterns, 'Spirit' carries a breezy hoedown feel, augmented by a splash of country viola that lightens the arrangement and gives it a rustic, almost Appalachian edge. The track moves at a fair pace, nimble and dexterous, and its arrangement is notably sophisticated, weaving acoustic textures around a steady backbeat.

Lyrically, Johnston leans toward the opaque, but the underlying message – perseverance, self-belief, a kind of gentle resilience – comes through. Everything is immaculately played and the band show restraint where they might once have opted for bombast. Yet, despite these strengths, the song doesn't quite lodge itself emotionally in the listener's memory. It feels like a deep cut left over from *Toulouse Street*: elegant, competently executed, but slightly unfinished. Its greatest merit is the glimpse it offers into Johnston's more introspective side, a quality often overshadowed by his muscular riffing.

'Pursuit On 53rd St.' (Johnston)

If 'Spirit' suggests moderation, then 'Pursuit On 53rd St.' swings hard in the opposite direction. Here, Tom Johnston reclaims his territory with a raucous, barely restrained rocker that feels like a cousin to 'China Grove'. The riffs are jagged, the tempo relentless and the vocal delivery borders on unhinged. It is short, sharp and more than a little mad. Bill Payne once again shows his value as a session player of rare brilliance, his piano parts cutting through the chaos with wit and precision. The whole affair feels like a moment of catharsis, the band deliberately cutting loose. One can't help but wonder if Johnston had absorbed Bob Seger's *Back In '72*, particularly 'Rosalie', whose rough-and-ready barroom punch seems like a clear precedent. Here, though, the Doobies apply their own gloss: tighter harmonies, cleaner production, but still the same barbed energy. The result is exhilarating if somewhat derivative – a vivid palate cleanser that prevents the record from settling too comfortably.

'Black Water' (Simmons)

Released as a single (with B-side 'Another Park, Another Sunday') in November 1974. Charts: US: 1.

Featured on Best Of The Doobies (1976)

'Black Water' is perhaps Pat Simmons' most defining contribution to The Doobie Brothers. It was the band's first number one on the *Billboard* Hot 100, despite being first released as a single ten months after its parent album and after reaching a high of number 32 as the B-side of 'Another Park, Another Sunday'. It's the very definition of a sleeper hit and one of the best songs recorded by this band.

'Black Water' stands as a quietly subversive moment in The Doobies' musical development – and more generally in mid-1970s rock – as it eschews bombast in favour of finger picked acoustic textures, sawing fiddle lines, gospel-tinged harmonies and a distinctly Southern, almost mythic imagery. Such ingredients were, at the time, something of an anomaly in the mainstream rock landscape. The song's languid, riverboat sway demonstrated Pat Simmons' instinct for fusing the familiar with the unexpected. His knack for acoustic storytelling brought a tonal richness to 'Black Water' and the wide Doobies' oeuvre that might otherwise have tilted too far towards polished pop or guitar-driven bluster.

'I was into folk blues,' Simmons told *Vintage Guitar*, 'and had that riff – kind of a lazy delta blues thing – to start. Soon after, I was in the studio, recording a part, and while they worked on something in the booth, I started playing that riff, just tweaking around. Our producer, Ted Templeman, said, 'What is that? There's something about that riff that's really cool.' So I continued to play with it. Shortly after, we were playing some shows in New Orleans when the song started to come to me. I think it was all the wonderful experiences – the food, walking along the Mississippi, the French Quarter, Dixieland music in the clubs. For instance, I wrote the second verse while riding a streetcar up St. Charles Street to the Garden District to do my laundry. It was raining – one of those summer showers where it's sunny. It was a magical moment for me.'

'I didn't play a note on that song,' Tom Johnston said in 2011. 'I just sang on it. That wasn't unusual in those days, actually – you could say the same thing about 'China Grove', Pat didn't really play on that song, I just went in and layered guitars. 'Black Water' was an unusual song – a place we'd never really gone before, with that round in the middle with the singing. Obviously, we'd been using finger picking for a while, but not with that kind of a rhythm behind it. It was pretty cool.'

The song culminates in a deftly arranged *a cappella* interlude with an infectious 'I'd like to hear some funky Dixieland' chorus that remains the song's most inspired flourish: a simulated jazz band rendered entirely through vocal harmony, at once playful and transcendent. Its success speaks not only to the Doobies' versatility but also to Simmons' ability to marry folk textures with mainstream appeal. It's a marvellous moment, not just for The Doobie Brothers, but for American music in the 1970s.

Pat Simmons admits that 'Black Water' was inspired by the Kenny Loggins song 'Long Tail Cat' (from 1972's *Loggins & Messina*). Both songs sit at the crossroads of folk, rock and Southern Americana, with acoustic textures, strong vocal harmonies, a rhythmic charm and an appealing communal, porch-jam feel. They differ in tone ('Black Water' is brisker, smoother and more sensual; 'Long Tail Cat' is quirky and playful), but they share a musical language rooted in American folk traditions and 1970s soft-rock fusion. 'Long Tail Cat' didn't make number one, however.

'Eyes Of Silver' (Johnston)

Released as a single (with B-side 'You Just Can't Stop It') in June 1974. Charts: US: 52.

Released in June 1974 as the lead single, 'Eyes Of Silver' was intended as the next big hit. On paper, it had everything: a driving Johnston riff, crisp drumming, Bill Payne's organ, a brass section adding colour and a vocal hook designed for radio play. And yet, it stalled at number 52. The reason is not difficult to discern: it is simply too close in spirit to 'Long Train Runnin'' to stand on its own. Producer Ted Templeman was clearly attempting to capture lightning in a bottle for the second time, but what was once fresh now felt formulaic. The parts are all in place, and the musicianship is flawless, but there is a sense of déjà vu that the public picked up on. In hindsight, 'Eyes Of Silver' is not without charm – its swaggering energy and Memphis Horns accents still entertain – but it lacks the originality of the band's stronger material. Its commercial disappointment paved the way for the surprise ascent of 'Black Water', which would eclipse it entirely.

'Road Angel' (Hartman, Hossack, Johnston, Porter)
Here is The Doobie Brothers at their most muscular. 'Road Angel' barrels down the highway with a confidence bordering on cocky, fuelled by the double-drumming of John Hartman and Michael Hossack, whose locked-in power provides the track with unstoppable momentum. Johnston's guitar snarls, Tiran Porter's bass drives like a freight train and Eddie Guzman's congas add a rhythmic elasticity that lifts the track above mere bluster. There is a Southern rock edge here, almost ZZ Top in its swagger, with twin-guitar harmonies that nod toward Thin Lizzy. Yet, the breakdown section is what truly elevates it: Johnston slashing at his rhythm guitar and the percussionists layering textures with a tight, driving drum kit, shakers and tambourine, and congas and other hand drums dropping in off-beat accents. The groove tightens until it explodes back into full-throttle motion. This is music designed for sweaty concert halls and open-road stereos. It may not possess the lyrical sophistication of Pat Simmons' work, but in sheer energy and execution, it is irresistible.

'You Just Can't Stop It' (Simmons)
Pat Simmons once again proves his range with this unexpected gem: a gospel-funk workout dressed in disco trappings. Sung with gusto by Tom Johnston, 'You Just Can't Stop It' brims with rhythmic verve. Bill Payne's clavinet adds a groovy bounce, the horns are arranged with real flair and Eddie Guzman's congas drive the beat with precision. The call-and-response vocal lines lend the track a communal spirit, as though the band were determined to prove they could hold their own in the funk arena. It is, in essence, a party captured on tape. What could easily have been a novelty instead becomes one of the album's most infectious moments. The Doobies are often remembered for their blend of rock and pop, but here they demonstrate a facility for cross-genre playfulness. In retrospect, it also strengthens the case for Simmons as the band's hidden genius, able to imagine and deliver material far outside their established comfort zone.

'Tell Me What You Want (And I'll Give You What You Need)'
(Simmons)
This is Pat Simmons at his most eclectic. Drawing on modal tunings, decorated by Jeff Baxter's pedal steel, Milt Holland's tabla and an autoharp

cameo by Arlo Guthrie, 'Tell Me What You Want…' presents a delicate tapestry of folk textures with a faintly psychedelic air. The arrangement is lush without being cluttered, drifting dreamily from verse to chorus. Yet, for all its beauty, the song lacks a fully resolved hook. The verses shimmer, Simmons delivering them with conviction, but the chorus arrives almost apologetically, never quite lifting the song into the memorable heights it seems to promise. One suspects it was an older piece resurrected to round out the album, and though it entertains in the moment, it does not linger long afterwards. Still, it is a testament to the band's willingness to experiment with instrumentation and atmosphere, even if the results fall slightly short.

'Down In The Track' (Johnston)

Tom Johnston digs deep into blues-boogie territory here, turning in a track laced with menace. The shuffle rhythm is relentless, and his voice has a rawness not always present in his more polished material. The lyrics paint impressionistic sketches of poverty, alienation and struggle – unusual subject matter for the band, who more often celebrate motion and escape than dwell on hardship. James Booker's piano adds a New Orleans authenticity, his flourishes darting around the central groove like sparks. The band attack the piece with admirable force, making it easy to imagine its power in a live setting. Yet, despite its strengths, the track carries a faint whiff of repetition, echoing earlier glories without quite surpassing them. It is a solid entry, but not a definitive one.

'Another Park, Another Sunday' (Johnston)

Released as a single (with B-side 'Black Water') in March 1974. Charts: US: 32.

The follow-up single to 'Long Train Runnin'', 'Another Park, Another Sunday' is perhaps just too low-key (or complex) to be an obvious hit. It takes a long time to get to its chorus. It's a breakup song disguised as an easy-going strum-along, blending melancholy lyrics with lush harmonies. It's beautifully constructed, emotionally accessible and one of the band's most graceful moments. Pat Simmons' guitar solo is gorgeous, wide open and effortlessly melodic. Tiran Porter's elegant, high-register bass playing underpins the melody. Porter also plays guitar through a rotating Leslie speaker, and Milt Holland's vibraphones add a summery feeling. 'That was an underrated tune', Pat Simmons said in 2025. 'We had high hopes for it as a single. It's one of my favourite tracks from that album.' Though commercially overshadowed, the track has aged gracefully, standing now as one of the band's most heartfelt moments. And of course, its B-side, 'Black Water', would ultimately rewrite the narrative.

'Daughters Of The Sea' (Simmons)

Pat Simmons leads the band into unexpected waters with this curiously structured piece. At once folk ballad, Celtic chant and proto-yacht rock, it unfolds through shifting time signatures and lyrics that evoke myth rather than autobiography. There is a touch of progressive rock here – Yes at their most pastoral, perhaps – but filtered through The Doobies' more grounded musicianship. The execution is impressive: the playing intricate, the arrangement balanced, the mood evocative. Yet, there remains a sense of detachment, as though the experiment were more intellectually satisfying than emotionally resonant. It is a fascinating glimpse of an alternate trajectory for the band, had they pursued a more esoteric, prog-influenced path, but ultimately feels more like an interlude than a core statement.

'Flying Cloud' (Porter)

The album closes with quiet grace. Tiran Porter's instrumental 'Flying Cloud' is brief but beautiful, a piece of impressionism rendered in guitar and bass. The atmosphere is airy, slightly mysterious, with the sense of a cinematic fade to black. The whole band contribute to its texture, showing their collective gift for restraint and space. Porter proves himself more than a bassist here, delivering a composition of delicacy and poise. As an ending, it is wholly fitting: reflective, understated and gently wistful. For those who only know the band through their greatest hits, it remains an undiscovered gem and one that encapsulates the breadth of their ambition on this record.

Stampede (1975)

Personnel:
Tom Johnston: vocals, guitars
Patrick Simmons: vocals, guitars
Jeff 'Skunk' Baxter: guitars, pedal steel guitar
Tiran Porter: bass, backing vocals
John Hartman: drums, percussion
Keith Knudsen: drums, percussion, vocals
With:
Bill Payne: piano, organ, electric piano
Ry Cooder: bottleneck guitar
Karl Himmel: drums and percussion
Bobbye Hall Porter: congas
Victor Feldman: marimba, percussion
Conte Candoli, Pete Candoli: trumpets
Maria Muldaur, Sherlie Matthews, Venetta Fields and Jessica Smith: backing vocals
Recorded at Warner Bros. Studios, North Hollywood, California; Burbank Studios, Burbank, California; Curtom Studios, Chicago; The Record Plant, Sausalito, California; and Creative Workshop, Nashville, between September and October 1974
Produced by Ted Templeman
Released: 25 April 1975
Highest chart positions: US: 4, UK: 14

The Doobie Brothers returned to the UK in July 1974 to play at that year's Knebworth Festival in front of 60,000 punters, mid-way down a bill headlined by The Allman Brothers Band. By now, their number had swollen to six with the addition of ex-Steely Dan guitar player Skunk Baxter, who had guested on *Toulouse Street* and *What Were Vices Are Now Habits*. 'Jeff (Skunk) was looking for some gigs with us,' Pat Simmons said a few years later, 'and he didn't even want to get paid. 'I just wanna get out and play for an audience', he said. 'Let me jam with you – I just wanna turn my guitar up and blast.' We were all getting disillusioned at the time… Jeff kicked us all in the ass.'

This lineup recorded just one album, *Stampede*, which, in hindsight, is the last great moment of the band's first act. It's an album of enormous musical breadth, enviable studio craft and the first signs of seismic change. If *What Were Once Vices* hinted at musical expansion, *Stampede* makes no secret of it. Here, the Doobies dive into country, funk, soul, swing and even mariachi. It's their most musically diverse album and, at times, their most disjointed. But there are riches here, and a sense that the band were ready to try anything, even if not all of it stuck. *Stampede*'s range is astonishing: country, funk, gospel, soul, orchestral rock and acoustic rags all coexist in relative harmony. There's a sense of a band unafraid to throw everything at the wall, not because they're unsure about what they want to say or how they want to be perceived, but because they're bursting with ideas.

Just ahead of the album's release, The Doobie Brothers visited Europe again in early 1975 as part of the legendary nine-city, 18-show tour of Germany, France, the Netherlands and the UK known as the Warner Brothers Music Show. Six bands would perform in various combinations, three each night: The Doobie Brothers, Tower of Power, Montrose, Little Feat, Graham Central Station and Bonaroo (featuring ex-Doobie Michael Hossack). Legend had it, and recordings attest, that Little Feat upstaged everyone. Elton John joined The Doobie Brothers for 'Listen To The Music' at The Free Trade Hall in Manchester on 16 January. *The Old Grey Whistle Test* covered the tour and broadcast an 11-minute live version of 'Without You', originally from *The Captain And Me*, recorded at The Rainbow in London. They returned to the US to play before 60,000 fans at the largest benefit concert held so far: the SNACK Benefit in San Francisco on 23 March. In a bill headlined by Bob Dylan, Neil Young, Joan Baez and Jefferson Starship, The Doobies played in the mid-afternoon after sets by Graham Central Station, Grateful Dead, Tower of Power and Santana. Not bad for $5.

At that show, The Doobie Brothers performed 'Take Me In Your Arms (Rock Me A Little While)' and 'I Been Working On You' from their soon-to-be-released new album. Yet, as the album came out a couple of weeks later, Tom Johnston would be forced to leave The Doobie Brothers, at least temporarily, after being admitted to hospital. It was 9 April in Baton Rouge, Louisiana, just before a scheduled concert, when Johnston was taken to Los Angeles for immediate treatment. He was 27, the same age that Jimi Hendrix, Janis Joplin and Jim Morrison had died from an excess of rock 'n' roll.

Remembers Pat Simmons: 'About that time, Tommy started to get ill on the road. He was developing stomach ulcers and was generally zinging out and couldn't handle the whole thing. We were doing between 150 and 200 dates a year at that point – a heavy-duty schedule, working all the time. We thought, 'Well, here goes the lead singer and we're going to have to pick up the pieces."

'My health was becoming a problem on and off…' Johnston wrote. 'The constant touring and wild lifestyle that went with it eventually caused the ulcer attacks to become more frequent.' The situation was more serious than anyone realised. 'I came close to dying', Johnston admitted in his memoirs. 'They lost me there for a few. No heartbeat.'

The band went on to play in Baton Rouge that night. Eventually, after several shows as a five-piece, Jeff Baxter placed a call to an ex-colleague. Enter Michael McDonald and, with him, a new sound, a new direction and a new chapter entirely.

Stampede stands as the last hurrah of the original Doobies – a band still riding with both wheels on the road, just before the terrain changed beneath them.

'Sweet Maxine' (Johnston, Simmons)
Released as a single (with B-side 'Double Dealin' Four Flusher') in July 1975. Charts: US: 40.
Opening with a honky-tonk piano riff and Tom Johnston in full vocal swagger, 'Sweet Maxine' is pure good-time rock 'n' roll, with multiple guitars and a piano part that could have rolled straight out of a Little Richard B-side (or lifted from Little Feat's 'Oh! Atlanta'). The song is loose, joyful and slightly throwaway, which may explain why it's aged so well: country boogie meets barroom brass. It's a rare co-write, with music by Pat Simmons and lyrics by Tom Johnston. Johnston: 'Just a great-feeling song with some really cool half-time sections and great chord changes.' The single version is heavily edited with some sections trimmed and a much earlier fade-out.

'Neal's Fandango' (Simmons)
Patrick Simmons' homage to author Neal Cassady (via Jack Kerouac) is one of this album's highlights. It's rooted in a breezy country-rock Moby Grape shuffle and is decorated with Jeff Baxter's ever-tasteful pedal steel guitar. Simmons sings that it's 'a windin' road I'm on, you understand', but the song is really about spiritual motion as opposed to physical motion. The reference to Loma Prieta in the chorus refers to a peak in the Santa Cruz Mountains of California. 'Neal's Fandango' is literate, catchy and warmly rendered – a road song for the bookshelf crowd.

'Texas Lullaby' (Johnston)
Tom Johnston tries his hand at a widescreen ballad, with mixed results. There's ambition here – strings, steel guitar, harmonies – but the song never quite transcends its influences (the slower songs of Lynyrd Skynyrd and The Allman Brothers Band, for example). The lyrics are oddly leaden ('Sittin' under an old oak tree, pickin' my guitar in the shade/That old tree spreadin' over my head is the closest friend I made') and the tempo plods rather than lopes. Jeff Baxter plays the swooping pedal steel and the jazzy acoustic guitar solo, and Bill Payne shines on piano.

'Music Man' (Johnston)
This is a something of a throwback track, steeped in blues and Southern soul. Tom Johnston delivers a loose-limbed vocal over a lazy funk groove. The coup here is the presence of Curtis Mayfield, who adds wah-wah guitar and arranged the horns, strings and backing singers (The Blackberries, who later sang on Pink Floyd's 'Shine On You Crazy Diamond'). Bill Payne adds B3. The bonkers guitar solo, which fades at the end of the song, is a mix of three passes, each by Tom Johnston, one of them played in reverse. The band work here as musical craftsmen, not hit makers – and that's not a criticism. This isn't the Doobies of 'Listen To The Music' – this is the Doobies of *Soul Train*.

'Slack Key Soquel Rag' (Simmons)

This charming instrumental interlude (incorrectly listed on first pressings of the album and on the B-side of 'Take Me In Your Arms (Rock Me A Little While)' as 'Slat Key Soquel Rag') was written and performed by Pat Simmons on acoustic guitar. The title nods to slack-key Hawaiian guitar traditions, though the tune itself is closer to folk-picking than island music. Some of the chord changes are outrageous with ragtime-inflected turnarounds and bright, attention-grabbing switches that momentarily yank the harmony sideways. It's brief, sub-two minutes, but beautifully recorded and stands as a delightful palate cleanser before the album's most unexpected turn.

'Take Me In Your Arms (Rock Me)' (Holland, Dozier, Holland)

Released as a single (with B-side 'Slat Key Soquel Rag') in April 1975. Charts: US: 11. UK: 29.

Featured on Best Of The Doobies (1976)

The big hit from the album is a cover version. It was written by the immortal Motown team of Holland-Dozier-Holland and originally recorded by Kim Weston. This was a bold choice for the band, but both Tom Johnston and Pat Simmons admired soul music and were only gradually building these influences into their own songs. 'I had been pushing the band to cover one of my favourite Motown tracks', Johnston recalled. 'The band played the hell out of it after we figured out the arrangement.'

The whole band lean into the groove with confidence. Bill Payne shines again, this time playing piano, and The Blackberries add their distinctive backing vocals. The guitar solo is sublime, pure Jeff Baxter; gloriously greasy. It's the best cover the Doobies ever did and a genuine pop-soul triumph. If your foot is not tapping, check your pulse. It's also a career pivot in disguise: as this song climbed the singles charts in April 1975,the band's future, Michael McDonald, was already performing with them, singing this song every night and bringing the house down.

Note: the song is incorrectly titled 'Take Me In Your Arms (Rock Me)' on this album and *Best Of The Doobies,* but is revised on some later compilations and live albums as 'Take Me In Your Arms (Rock Me A Little While)'.

'I Cheat The Hangman' (Simmons)

Released as a single (with B-side 'Music Man') in November 1975. Charts: US: 60.

This is the album's most ambitious track by far. Pat Simmons channels ghost-story mysticism over a brooding intro that builds into an orchestral crescendo – half Ennio Morricone, half *Abbey Road*. The song weaves a tale inspired by Ambrose Bierce's short story *An Occurrence At Owl Creek Bridge*. In Simmons' telling – or rather, his retelling – the protagonist is a Civil War ghost who returns to his home, unaware of his own demise. Simmons himself said it 'has the feel of an old west ghost town' and explicitly acknowledged the Bierce influence. It is an atmospheric oddity that could be a gothic short story.

Musically, 'I Cheat The Hangman' departs dramatically from the standard blues-rock fare of the era. The first four-and-a-half minutes of the track layer guitars, piano, crust-and-bones vocals, bass and drums before morphing into timpani, strings, ominous harmonies and a rising sense of dread. This grand, ghost-choir crescendo was conceived with arranger Nick DeCaro, whose vision was partly inspired by Mussorgsky's *Night On Bald Mountain*. 'I Cheat The Hangman' is not an easy listen, but it's utterly compelling. The Doobies, briefly, go symphonic – and Warner Bros. released it as a single!

'Précis' (Baxter)

This brief, semi-classical acoustic guitar solo by Jeff Baxter is elegant, refined and utterly unnecessary, and was surely included merely as a sop. It impresses, sure, but breaks the spell after 'I Cheat The Hangman'.

'Rainy Day Crossroad Blues' (Johnston)

A return to basics. Tom Johnston delivers a finger picked acoustic blues tune with tasteful slide guitar (Ry Cooder, natch) and harmonica. It's easy to overlook this track, but it's one of the more emotionally direct on the album. Stripped of production tricks, Johnston reveals himself as the Doobies' most grounded songwriter – wistful, melodic and utterly unpretentious. The change after two minutes is as welcome as it is surprising: the tempo drops, the pedal steel sings, the strings swell. Glorious.

'I Been Workin' On You' (Johnston)

A detour into funk-soul territory with a heavy Stax influence, 'I Been Workin' On You' started as a jam before being worked on and recorded by Tom Johnston, Tiran Porter and their friend Karl Himmel, the drummer with Mother Earth (who had toured with The Doobies a few years before). Johnston added a growling guide vocal, which was used in the final mix, and overdubbed a belligerent guitar solo which rises and flies. The soulful backing singers soften and sweeten an attractively simple tune which looks backwards to 1960s soul music and forwards to The Doobies of the late 1970s in equal measure.

'Double Dealin' Four Flusher' (Simmons)

The album closes on a swaggering Southern-rock style shuffle with brassy punctuation and a tale of romantic betrayal. The title sounds like something out of a 1930s pulp novel, and the music matches: theatrical, tongue-in-cheek and knowingly over the top. Bill Payne plays some fruity piano, and if you listen hard, you can identify three lead singers: Pat Simmons, Keith Knudsen and Tom Johnston. And then, after two minutes, it drops away into jazzy noodling before picking up the pace to take it home.

If *Toulouse Street* and *The Captain And Me* had already proved The Doobie Brothers could straddle both denim-clad boogie and radio-friendly melody, then *Stampede* pushed the boundaries out into uncharted pastures: the seismic change of the band's next release would be much more of a shock had *Stampede* not provided the musical Vaseline between the band's fourth and sixth albums.

Takin' It To The Streets (1976)

Personnel:
Tom Johnston: vocals, guitars
Patrick Simmons: vocals, guitars
Jeff 'Skunk' Baxter: guitars
Michael McDonald: vocals, piano, electric piano, clavinet, synthesisers
Tiran Porter: bass, vocals
John Hartman: drums, percussion
Keith Knudsen: drums, percussion, backing vocals
With:
Wayne Jackson: trumpet
Andrew Love: tenor saxophone
James Mitchell: baritone saxophone
Lewis Collins: tenor saxophone
Jack Hale: trombone
Bobby LaKind: congas
Richie Hayward: drums
Novi Novog: viola
Jesse Butler: organ
Maria Muldaur: vocals
Ted Templeman: percussion
Recorded at Warner Bros. Studios, North Hollywood and Sunset Sound, Los Angeles, in 1975
Produced by Ted Templeman
Released 19 March 1976
Highest chart positions: US: 8, UK: 42

> You can lead a Doobie to the recording studio, but you can't make him think. C+
> **Robert Christgau, *Village Voice*, reviewing *Takin' It To The Streets* (1976)**

Takin' It To The Streets **introduces Michael McDonald to The Doobie Brothers. McDonald, who grew up in the suburbs of St. Louis, heard Ray Charles and The Beatles in High School. 'My Aunt Ann Catherine's… record collection included Ray Charles's *Modern Sounds In Country And Western Music*', he wrote in his memoirs, 'I would lie on the floor of her apartment, close my eyes and listen to that album on repeat for hours on end. There was something undeniable in his melodic interpretation, vocal performances that you just knew were purely inspired in the moment and likely to never be repeated exactly the same way again, the way he mined the hidden poignancy of the lyrics. I couldn't have explained it at the time. I just knew after hearing Ray Charles, I would never be the same.'**

He learned a few chords on guitar and formed his first band, Mike and the Majestics, aged 12. 'Mike and the Majestics started like most bands,' he wrote,

'close to home. We'd rehearse in our drummer's basement after school, playing the only three songs we knew: 'Boys', 'Rock And Roll Music' and 'Money' [both from the first two albums by The Beatles], which all sounded uncannily similar when we played them. These, of course, were originally American R&B songs that only came to us by way of The Beatles. At this point in my 'career', I was just trying to imitate the singers I heard on the recordings … while I like to think I could decently carry a tune back then, it's safe to say that whatever vocal qualities one might associate with my singing today, they for sure hadn't developed yet.'

A chance hearing of 'Stop Her On Sight (SOS)' by Edwin Starr caught his attention. 'The musical and rhythmic sophistication spoke to me', he wrote later. 'It was something beyond the more simplistic, folkish reinvention of American soul music we were digging by the British bands.'

He subsequently joined Jerry Jay and the Sheratons as vocalist, performing classic and contemporary rhythm and blues in the greater St. Louis area, then periods with the Reeb Toors, the Delrays (who released a single called 'Lollipop Lady' in 1968; the B-side is a thrilling version of 'Always Something There To Remind Me') and The Guild. It was when he was playing with a band called Blue that he met Rick Jarrard, who had produced Jefferson Airplane's *Surrealistic Pillow* (1967), Harry Nilsson's *Aerial Ballet* (1968) and José Feliciano's *Feliciano!* (1968). Jarrard had heard a demo of two of Blue's original songs and wanted to sign McDonald to a solo deal.

'So, in August 1970,' McDonald wrote, 'before what would have been my senior year in high school, I happily accepted the plane ticket RCA sent me – and the $3,000 advance, most of which I gave my mom to keep the house running in the absence of my gig income – and packed up for California. Before I got on the plane, I called a couple of people to say goodbye, and when one of my friends asked, 'So, when are you gonna be back?', it was only then that it hit me. 'Um ... I don't know that I am coming back.' I hadn't thought it through that far. I could see only what was immediately in front of me: I was gonna get on that plane and go to California to make a record.'

On the first day of sessions, McDonald recorded 'Take Me To The Pilot' by the then-unknown writing duo of Elton John and Bernie Taupin. The album comprised McDonald's original songs but was not released and remains unheard. A second was also recorded but is also unreleased. McDonald spent the next several years as a live performer, session player and songwriter for hire: he wrote a song for and played piano on David Cassidy's UK number one album *Dreams Are Nuthin' More Than Wishes* (1973), amongst others.

He crossed paths with drummer Jeff Porcaro, who was starting to build a reputation as the go-to session drummer in Los Angeles. Porcaro had played on a track on Steely Dan's album *Pretzel Logic*. Some months later, in March 1974, Porcaro agreed to join Steely Dan for an upcoming tour and suggested McDonald as a keyboard player/backing vocalist. 'Jeff… recommended me, which blew my mind!' McDonald wrote. 'He was actually calling from their rehearsal to ask if I wanted to audition. I said, 'Sure! When?' And he said, 'How about now?' I threw my Wurlitzer into my Ford Pinto and hauled my ass down to Modern Music rentals and rehearsals in Hollywood.'

The tour lasted for three months, during which time McDonald became friendly with Steely Dan's guitarist Jeff 'Skunk' Baxter. Walter Becker and Donald Fagen dismantled the live lineup of Steely Dan when the tour ended in July 1974. Jeff Baxter promptly joined The Doobie Brothers in time for *Stampede*. That album's three singles had mixed results. Although 'Take Me In Your Arms (Rock Me A Little While)' had reached a high of number 11, 'Sweet Maxine' barely reached the top 40 and 'I Cheat The Hangman' stopped at number 60. A few days into a seven-week tour, which started in April 1975, Tom Johnston was sidelined with a serious ulcer.

Pat Simmons: 'Jeff Baxter pulled me aside backstage one night… 'Hey man, remember that guy we had singing background in Steely Dan?' I had a vague recollection… I wasn't sure what to think, but Jeff was adamant. A few days later, a shaggy-haired, bearded background singer arrived from LA.'

'Somewhere along the way, [Jeff Baxter] got word to me that the Doobies might have a temporary need for my services on keyboard and vocals,' McDonald recalled. 'It was a moment of almost unheard-of good fortune that I was invited to step on the deck of this already phenomenally successful musical enterprise. The catch was I had to be on a plane the next morning to fly to New Orleans and go right into rehearsal. With just two days' rehearsal, I managed to get a handle on all of the Doobies' roughly two-hour-long show, taking sufficient notes, but more so tapping into my years of club experience, which did come in handy here. I'd become a quick study and developed a somewhat enhanced power of retention. Two days. That was it.'

'I wasn't sure what to expect,' noted Tiran Porter, 'but I will tell you, the second I heard him open his mouth, I said holy shit. My mind was blown right there.'

McDonald, who had just turned 23, played his first show with The Doobie Brothers at the Hirsch Memorial Coliseum, Shreveport, Louisiana, on 11 April 1975. He had no expectation that the gig would last past the end of the current run of live dates, which ended in Canada on 21 May. But, when the tour ended and recording sessions were booked, The Doobie Brothers took Michael McDonald into the studio, subsequently asking him to be a permanent member. Tom Johnston remained with the band, for now, and wrote 'Turn It Loose' for *Takin' It To The Streets*, as well as singing with Pat Simmons on 'Wheels Of Fortune'. Michael McDonald put forward some of his own songs, including the title track, a big hit in the spring of 1976, and 'It Keeps You Runnin'', which also reached the top 40.

'The *Takin' It To The Streets* album was recorded in the summer of '75,' McDonald noted, 'our first experience of long, extended night sessions – trying to get as much done as possible before we hit the road again. I remember having to take catnaps on the floor of the studio, trying to catch up on lost sleep.'

Takin' It To The Streets masterfully bridges the old and the new, showcasing the band's evolution from their raw early sound to a more refined and sophisticated style. At this moment and on this album, they stood confidently, straddling the past and the future.

Although he plays and sings on *Takin' It To The Streets* (and would remain a full member of the band until early 1977), Tom Johnston had one foot out of the door. 'I don't know that I'm the person to speak to the matter of his possible ambivalence about this project', Michael McDonald later admitted. 'On the other hand, I couldn't help but feel somehow responsible. The group that he had founded with Pat and then left for a short while had changed – not surprisingly, since his contribution and presence had always had such a formidable impact. So his absence was palpable to any ardent Doobie Brothers fan. His voice and songs had been – and always will be – such a signature of the band's sound. So in that temporary vacuum, a shift of sorts was inevitable.'

Their music retained a wide base of appeal, but rather than the organic mix of Johnston's upbeat, guitar-driven sound and Simmons' touches of folk, bluegrass, country and Dixieland, it would be a combination of Simmons' music explorations with a shift toward sophisticated, studio-refined production, mostly keyboard-based and with the rich, emotive baritone blue-eyed soul vocals of Michael McDonald.

McDonald, for his part, continued to record with Steely Dan, adding his distinctive backing vocals to three songs from *Katy Lied* ('Doctor Wu', 'Any World (That I'm Welcome To)' and 'Bad Sneakers'), three from *The Royal Scam* ('Kid Charlemagne', 'Don't Take Me Alive' and 'The Fez'), two from *Aja* ('I Got The News' and the exquisite 'Peg') and one from *Gaucho* ('Hey Nineteen'). He also toured as Randy Newman's musical director in 1977.

'Wheels Of Fortune' (Simmons, Baxter, Hartman)

Released as a single (with B-side 'Slat Key Soquel Rag') in August 1976. Charts: US: 87

The album's opener finds a three-way composition by Patrick Simmons, Jeff Baxter and John Hartman. They deliver a taut slice of funk-rock that reflects the socio-economic uncertainty of the era, though the groove suggests optimism rather than resignation. Horns punch through the mix, foreshadowing the R&B textures that Michael McDonald would soon cement as a trademark. Pat Simmons and Tom Johnston share lead vocals.

This was the first song that Michael McDonald recorded with The Doobie Brothers, recorded live in the studio, including solos for electric piano, guitar and saxophone. Little Feat's Richie Hayward sits in for an absent Keith Knudsen. This was also conga player Bobby LaKind's first recording with the band. He was part of the lighting crew and would sometimes get up on stage as an additional percussionist.

'Bobby told us he played the conga drums and asked if he could sit in and play on 'Listen To The Music' [during live shows]', Pat Simmons recalled.

'None of us thought this was a good idea. We put him off for a long time. But Bobby was persistent, and I think at some point we just gave in to get him off our backs. Well, lo and behold, he was pretty damn good. Then he wanted to play on other tunes. Well, finally we let him play on 'Long Train Runnin''. Suddenly, the song came alive. As far as I was concerned, he was a fantastic player and one of the best percussionists I've ever played with.' LaKind would officially join the band for two stints in the 1980s and co-write a number of songs in the years ahead. 'I'm not sure there were many other bands that ever promoted a roadie to band member', Simmons commented.

'Wheels Of Fortune' is an apt curtain-raiser: gritty and not without a sense of swagger. Almost 90 seconds were chopped from the middle of the song for the single version: the piano and guitar solos are significantly edited.

'Takin' It To The Streets' (McDonald)
Released as a single (with B-side 'For Someone Special') in March 1976. Charts: US: 13.
Featured on Best Of The Doobies (1976)

> A friend of mine told me about first hearing 'Takin' It To The Streets' on the radio. He was driving with a couple of his buddies, all of them already fans of the group. As the DJ announced, 'a new song by the Doobie Brothers!', he reached for his car radio in anticipation and cranked the volume. As the song's intro began, they all looked around at one another, perplexed ... till one of them broke the silence with 'What the fuck is that?'
> Michael McDonald, ***What A Fool Believes: A Memoir*** **(2024)**

Michael McDonald's debut as lead vocalist on a Doobie Brothers single is nothing short of revelatory. With its gospel-inflected piano chords and anthemic chorus, the title track is both a statement of intent and a master class in soulful economy. McDonald's voice, all velvet and gravel – that grainy, slightly raspy push with a super-smooth, almost smoky sheen – brings gravitas to a lyric that channels urban compassion and social consciousness – subjects often absent from mid-1970s FM rock.

McDonald: 'The original germ of the idea emerged from conversations I had with my younger sister… who, like most of her college-age contemporaries, had grown very socially conscious. A true product of their time, they were growing more keenly aware of things like rural and inner-city poverty, the exponential growth of economic disparity, the ever-increasing number of Americans falling through the ever-widening cracks… We would find ourselves talking about the hope of a more equitable society and the hard truth that progressive change like that historically never came easily. As idealistic and overly intellectualised as the subject may sound, it struck me… that it might be just the right lyric subject matter for this gospel-inspired chord progression I had been tinkering with. I had always wanted to write what I felt could pass for a traditional gospel song; that style always held a powerful attraction for me. Musically, I started with the piano intro/verse, followed by the ramp-up to the chorus, and the lyrics came pretty easily for those first two sections. For the chorus, I felt it should just kind of sing itself when I got there. However, initially, the title was elusive; 'Falling Through The Cracks' just wasn't gonna pay off. And… later… it came to me: 'Takin' It To The Streets'. By the time I got home that night, I all but had a new song.'

Built on a steady, gospel-leaning piano figure, the song moves with a deliberate, almost processional weight, giving McDonald's vocal space to push forward with that mix of grit and warmth he'd make his trademark. The harmony shifts are simple but purposeful, circling back to the tonic with a sense of resolve rather than repetition, while the horn lines and backing vocals add a firm, disciplined lift. It's a tighter, more urban sound than the band's earlier work and the arrangement underscores its message: a controlled, insistent groove carrying an argument that refuses to be brushed aside.

McDonald's original demo was released in 2000. This lays out the template for the song. 'When the band played it,' he told Bob Harris in 2025, 'it became a whole other animal. It was one of those moments that you never forget. And you're looking for that the rest of your life: you're hoping that you ever feel that way again.'

'8th Avenue Shuffle' (Simmons)

A curious hybrid of boogie and back-alley jazz-funk, '8th Avenue Shuffle' immediately sets itself apart as a track unafraid to roam between genres. The song's elasticity comes from the interplay between Simmons' earthy, almost conversational guitar lines and Jeff Baxter's signature fluid phrasing. Each lick carries his unmistakable tone – a slightly metallic shimmer layered with subtle wah nuances – that slices through the rhythm section with precision. Speaking of which, the bass and drums channel a Tower of Power-style funk mastery, locking in grooves that are complex enough to impress the most jaded listeners while remaining irresistibly danceable.

Lyrically, the track eschews narrative in favour of mood. Simmons' vocals are less concerned with storytelling than with enhancing the track's smoky, nocturnal atmosphere. There's a kind of conversational intimacy here, a sense that the band are jamming not just with each other but directly with the listener. The result is a track that feels alive and improvisational, a quiet testament to the Doobies' mid-career willingness to stretch beyond the expected.

'Losin' End' (McDonald)

'Losin' End' takes the listener to a markedly darker, more introspective space. Built on sparse minor chords and deliberate emotional restraint, the song finds Michael McDonald exploring romantic disappointment with a subtle, almost imperceptible melancholy. Strings thread quietly through the arrangement, lending a cinematic quality to the otherwise minimal instrumentation – a foreshadowing of the sophisticated balladry that would later become a McDonald hallmark. The track's beauty lies in its restraint. Each note and vocal inflection is weighted with intent; nothing is superfluous.

McDonald recalled the song's humble beginnings: 'I was having dinner one night at Tiran's house, and he said, 'Hey, come check out my little four-track recording studio. Maybe we can lay something down tonight.' We recorded something I was working on called 'Losin' End'. I had not written much by then. It was just kind of a little one-off I had done. Well, lo and behold, our producer, Ted Templeman, heard it and really liked it.'

'Rio' (Simmons, Baxter)

Pat Simmons' adventurous streak shines on 'Rio', a track that juxtaposes the bossa nova-inflected chordal structure with layered guitars that favour texture over traditional hooks. Here, Simmons demonstrates once again a willingness to push the Doobies' sonic boundaries, offering a left-field diversion from the band's California rock roots. Jeff Baxter's contributions enrich the tonal landscape, weaving shimmering guitar harmonics into the mix and accentuating the track's atmospheric qualities with jazzy extensions and tasteful chromatic touches. Lyrically, 'Rio' remains impressionistic, bordering on elusive. Both geographically and stylistically, 'Rio' is a long way from 'China Grove'.

'For Someone Special' (Porter)

'For Someone Special' is another change of pace. It was written and sung by Tiran Porter and is delicious jazz fusion with a bluesy aesthetic. It's a quietly unassuming gem, languid and subdued. Yet, within its simplicity lies a striking emotional clarity. The narrative voice is weary but resolute. There's no grand flourish here, only a soft resignation. Sonically, the track is uncluttered – there are no soaring solos or flamboyant arrangement tricks to distract. That restraint becomes the song's quiet strength: it mirrors the emotional landscape of acceptance rather than exaltation. In the broader arc of The Doobie Brothers' catalogue, 'For Someone Special' may not be a radio staple, but it is precisely the sort of deep track that rewards repeat listening.

'It Keeps You Runnin'' (McDonald)

Released as a single (with B-side 'Turn It Loose') in October 1976. Charts: US: 37. Featured on Best Of The Doobies (1976)

Built around a hypnotic keyboard riff and layered harmonies, 'It Keeps You Runnin'' is sleek, urbane and utterly assured. Michael McDonald described it as 'another life-changing composition.'

'That song was the miraculous result of my one day's attendance at the Dick Grove School of Music, a master class held in a small office space on Ventura

Boulevard', he writes. 'On that particular day, the instructor, Mr. Grove himself, who was an accomplished jazz pianist, was talking about passing chords and standard jazz chord progressions. He demonstrated how beautiful compositions, like Jerome Kern's 'All The Things You Are', are often built on what might technically be considered a series of passing chords, changing keys, creating the basic harmonic body of the song. That one-hour class kind of blew my mind wide open; almost every song I wrote after that – especially songs like 'It Keeps You Runnin'', with its chromatically descending II-V passing chord progression – was directly influenced by what I learned that day. As for the lyrics on that one, they were just about the fear of re-experiencing heartbreak in the past and the natural reluctance to ever letting oneself be vulnerable again.'

The song opens with a characteristic McDonald piano figure: gently syncopated, harmonically rich and already hinting at motion. The groove is steady but not hurried: John Hartman and Keith Knudsen keep it understated, almost deferential, allowing the harmonic tension to carry the momentum. The guitars – once the rhythmic engine of The Doobies – are now a colour rather than a framework, layered beneath McDonald's electric piano and the subtle wash of backing vocals.

Lyrically, the track is built around repetition. McDonald sketches the portrait of someone caught in a cycle of flight, unable or unwilling to pause and confront the cause. The refrain is not delivered as a command or accusation but as a weary observation, underscored by the longing in his delivery.

This track was first released by Carly Simon several months before *Takin' It To The Streets*. The Doobie Brothers play on her version, from the album *Another Passenger* (1976),and also a second track, 'Half A Chance', recorded on the same day. Yet, it's in this version that one hears the precise moment The Doobie Brothers' creative centre of gravity shifted – gently, but irrevocably – toward the reflective, groove-based sophistication that would define their next chapter.

'Turn It Loose' (Johnston)

Here is Tom Johnston's principal contribution to *Takin' It To The Streets*. 'Everybody had made me feel welcome,' Johnston recalled, 'and pitched in to make 'Turn It Loose' as good as it could be. The guys were all supportive, and Ted was welcoming as well. And while it felt very different working in the new band environment after all that they'd been through since I'd had to leave, I was grateful for the chance to be a part of it.'

'Turn It Loose' emerges as a personal, emotionally raw interjection within an album otherwise reshaped by Michael McDonald's soul-infused style. The title itself has a dual meaning. It could mean letting go of pain; it might mean letting go of preconceptions or expectations. In Johnston's weary delivery, it sounds like emancipation and resignation in the same breath. Lyrics such as 'I thought I had a grip on things/Now I just don't know' carry an urgency that's both universal and quietly heartbreaking. Instrumentally, the track stays grounded in The Doobies' familiar rock foundation – guitar, bass, steady rhythms – yet it's imbued with a tension which cannot be ignored.

Though not a single and unlikely to have enjoyed mainstream radio rotation, the song's inclusion reminds listeners that, beneath the band's gradual musical transformation, Tom Johnston was an integral part of The Doobie Brothers, even if one suspects that he knows that he has one foot out of the door.

'Carry Me Away' (Simmons, Baxter, McDonald)
There's a subtle restlessness captured in the melody of 'Carry Me Away'. It's a yearning not for dramatic escape, but for gentle elevation – a quiet hope that something, or someone, might lift you beyond the familiar. Michael McDonald's voice, with its velvet smoothness and steel-capped clarity, is the perfect vessel for that longing.

Instrumentally, the track is emblematic of The Doobie Brothers' mid-1970s transformation. Guitar lines from Pat Simmons and especially Jeff Baxter don't blaze in the tradition of the band's earlier rock songs; instead, they weave in and out, painting harmonic contours beneath McDonald's piano and soft horns. This layered approach – guitar as atmosphere, piano and voice at the heart – underlines the shift from the swagger of the band's early work toward a more urbane, reflective elegance.

Though not a single and often overshadowed by the album's more radio-friendly offerings, 'Carry Me Away' remains a quietly compelling footnote in the Doobies' catalogue, elegantly framed by restraint and nuanced performance.

Best Of The Doobies (1976)

Track list: 'China Grove', 'Long Train Runnin'', 'Takin' It To The Streets', 'Listen To The Music', 'Black Water', 'Rockin' Down The Highway', 'Jesus Is Just Alright', 'It Keeps You Runnin'', 'South City Midnight Lady', 'Take Me In Your Arms (Rock Me A Little While)', 'Without You'

Tom Johnston returned to The Doobie Brothers for a series of live dates in the spring of 1976 to discover the band had moved on without him. 'The 1976 tour… really represented both styles of the band', Johnston wrote in his memoirs. 'The crowd loved it because they got everything. We played a lot of the songs from before mixed in with the new tracks, but it did not feel like The Doobie Brothers I was accustomed to anymore, but rather what The Doobie Brothers had become. Michael's music was such a different direction for the band, but just as valid as anything we had done previously, and with this configuration, the band had moved on. They had a future, and as much as I respected where they were headed, I felt a little out of place.' Johnston's lively, rhythm-heavy style, long the group's signature, now felt out of step with the new material coming from his replacement. By the end of the year, he once again withdrew from touring.

Best Of The Doobies, released on 29 October 1976, neatly summarises his time with the band. It's not merely a contractual pit stop or a casual roundup of hits – it's a neatly sealed time capsule. It serves as a farewell letter (at least for the time being) to the original, denim-clad incarnation of the group: the boogie-loving, harmony-rich, guitar-driven ensemble that had risen from the bars of Northern California to the upper echelons of American rock radio. In that light, *Best Of The Doobies* may be viewed as both celebration and eulogy of the first six years of The Doobie Brothers: to their four top ten albums, six top 20 singles (all included here) and countless nights in bars, clubs, concert halls and arenas.

The song selection is impeccable – 12 songs, each a staple of '70s FM airwaves. There's a distinct unity to this collection, a sonic signature defined by Tom Johnston's throaty vocals, Patrick Simmons' folksy inclinations and a rhythm section that played like they'd been raised on Little Feat and Creedence in equal measure. One is struck by the cohesiveness of the material, especially considering the rapid evolution the band had already commenced. This is The Doobie Brothers rooted in tight harmonies, three-minute road anthems and a palpable sense of West Coast freedom. Even on tracks like 'Black Water', where Simmons stretches into acoustic territory with a dash of New Orleans, the mood is still resolutely earthy.

Viewed this way, the album's purpose becomes clearer: it offers the casual listener a tour of the first chapter, while quietly closing the door behind it. Tom Johnston's health issues had removed him from the touring lineup; Michael McDonald was no longer just a stand-in: he was the future. *Best Of The Doobies* is not just a collection of hits – it is a line in the sand.

Commercially, the album was a triumph, eventually going multi-platinum with more than 12 million sales. This is a testament to the band's mainstream appeal and ubiquity on American radio. But there's something poignant in that success, as though the band's original spirit had to be anthologised in order to survive what was coming next. For long-time fans, *Best Of The Doobies* served as reassurance: that whatever came after, however smoother, silkier or more Steely Dan-adjacent, it could never erase the raw, joyous energy of songs like 'Rockin' Down The Highway' or 'Listen To The Music'.

Tom Johnston officially left The Doobie Brothers in January 1977 during the early sessions for their next album, *Livin' On The Fault Line*. 'I had four songs ready for the album,' he said in 2011, 'but I pulled them off and said, 'I have to go for a while'... I left the band to get away from the road scene. Basically, we were either on the road or in the studio *all the time*. There wasn't any time at home, and I'm a homebody. So, I left. And all I did was play baseball and lift weights. I didn't really pick up a guitar for about six months, then I started slowly drifting back into it.'

Johnston released the first of two solo albums, *Everything You've Heard Is True* (produced by Ted Templeman), in December 1979. Pat Simmons, Michael McDonald, Keith Knudsen and Bill Payne all contribute. The single 'Savannah Nights' would top out at number 34 the following month.

Livin' On The Fault Line (1977)

Personnel:
Patrick Simmons: vocals, guitars
Jeff 'Skunk' Baxter: guitars
Michael McDonald: vocals, piano, organ, clavinet, synthesiser
Tiran Porter: bass, vocals
Keith Knudsen: drums, percussion, backing vocals
John Hartman: drums, percussion
With:
Bobby LaKind: congas, backing vocals
Dan Armstrong: electric sitar
Randy Brecker: trumpet
Norton Buffalo: harmonica
Victor Feldman: vibes
Rosemary Butler: backing vocals
Maureen McDonald: backing vocals
Ted Templeman: percussion
Recorded at Sunset Sound Recorders, Hollywood, Western Recorders, Hollywood and Warner Bros. Recording Studios, North Hollywood, in 1977
Produced by Ted Templeman
Released: 19 August 1977
Highest chart positions: US: 10, UK: 25

By the time *Livin' On The Fault Line* arrived in August 1977, The Doobie Brothers had undergone their two-year transformation. Gone was the bar-band boogie of *Toulouse Street* and *The Captain And Me*; in its place came something silkier, smoother and unmistakably urban. Pat Simmons continued to be the connective tissue between the Doobies' rough-hewn, guitar-driven roots and their sleek, soul-inflected new direction. His songs on this album – 'Echoes Of Love' and 'Chinatown' – maintained one half of the band's harmonic DNA while adapting gracefully to the more sophisticated production and jazz-influenced textures that Michael McDonald brought in.

McDonald: 'For a long time, people have said to me, 'You changed the Doobie Brothers. They adopted your sound.' But that's not true at all. It may be my voice on some of the songs, but it's the band that adapted everything, not just me. That's what's so great about the Doobies. It's a total band situation. Their sound evolved as a whole unit, not just because of me. They all wanted to try new things, and they did. Maybe my being there created some sort of opportunity to do things differently. But it was hardly me doing all the work. That was always a band of very talented musicians that always rose to the occasion.'

While *Livin' On The Fault Line* didn't yield the monster hits of its predecessors or successors, it is perhaps the Doobie Brothers' most overlooked record – and, in some ways, their most intriguing. It's a quiet storm of an album, defined more by mood than melody and more by groove than hooks. It's probably their least commercial. It doesn't shout for your attention (there are no hard, gutsy guitar tracks), but it waits for you to meet it halfway. For those expecting the exuberant sing-alongs of earlier albums, it may feel muted. But for those willing to listen, it rewards.

On the road, the band headlined the third night of that year's Reading Festival, on 28 August 1977, closing a typically eclectic day's entertainment comprising The Motors, The Enid, Hawkwind and Wayne County and the Electric Chairs.

Early in 1978, The Doobie Brothers appeared in a two-part episode of the popular sitcom *What's Happening!!* (ABC, 1976-1979), which followed the lives of working-class African-American teens living in the Los Angeles neighbourhood of Watts. 'Doobie Or Not Doobie (Parts 1 & 2)' saw the central characters, Raj, Rerun, Dwayne and Dee, getting free tickets to a Doobie Brothers concert. The catch? They have to secretly tape the show for a shady promoter who's bootlegging live performances. The Doobie Brothers confront the trio backstage, telling them (and the audience by proxy) about the seriousness of music piracy. It was part concert, part public service announcement, a little heavy-handed but well-intentioned. It includes an excellent (if abbreviated) 12-minute live performance comprising 'Black Water', 'Take Me In Your Arms (Rock Me A Little White)', 'I Cheat The Hangman' and a phenomenal version of 'Takin' It To The Streets', as well as some enthusiastically awful acting by the band.

What's Happening!! was a clever PR move that broadened the band's fan base, softened their image and kept them in the public eye during the run-up to their biggest commercial success. The subject matter gave them goodwill in the music business and in the press – it was seen as artists standing up for their livelihood without coming off as preachy. 'I don't think we appreciated at the time the effect that that show would have on our career,' Pat Simmons noted, 'but that was the power of television back then.' Both episodes are on YouTube at the time of writing.

'You're Made That Way' (McDonald, Baxter, Knudsen)

'You're Made That Way' sets the album's tone with a sleek, almost clinical sophistication. McDonald's hypnotic piano groove, layered with clavinet and synthesisers, immediately evokes mid-period Steely Dan – not at all inappropriate now that two ex-members were on board the Doobies' train. The song's cryptic lyrics contribute to the mood, emphasising texture and tonal intrigue over straightforward storytelling. The track exemplifies McDonald-era Doobies': introspective, rhythmically meticulous and highly produced.

'Echoes Of Love' (Simmons, Mitchell, Randle)

Released as a single (with B-side 'There's A Light') in September 1977. Charts: US: 66.
Featured on Best Of The Doobies Volume II (1981)

This is one of the few tracks on *Livin' On The Fault Line* with radio aspirations and is arguably the record's most immediate moment. It's co-written with Willie Mitchell and Earl Randle. Mitchell was a highly influential trumpeter, bandleader, arranger and record producer who developed the Memphis Soul sound of Al Green, Ann Peebles and others. Randle worked extensively with Willie Mitchell at Hi Records between 1971 and 1980. Evidently, 'Echoes Of Love' was offered to Al Green, who declined it – leading to Simmons adapting it for The Doobie Brothers.

Simmons handles lead vocals here, bringing a touch of warmth to the mid-tempo shuffle. The harmonies are buttery, the production immaculate. It's a love song, but not an effusive one – there's restraint here, typical of the album as a whole. The song also exemplifies the band's stylistic shift since 1975: although Simmons writes and sings, it could easily be Michael McDonald's work.

Released as the second single from the album, it stalled at number 66. 'Echoes Of Love' was later covered by The Pointer Sisters on their 1978 album *Energy*. The two groups also performed it together in concert and on TV.

'Little Darling (I Need You)' (Holland, Dozier, Holland)

Released as a single (with B-side 'Losin' End') in July 1977. Charts: US: 48, UK: 50.

Featured on Best Of The Doobies Volume II (1981)

This Motown cover feels redundant, despite Michael McDonald's best Marvin Gaye impression. One gets the feeling that the band and/or producer said, 'We need a single…'

'Little Darling (I Need You)' was written and produced by Holland, Dozier and Holland (composers of 'Take Me In Your Arms (Rock Me A Little While)') and recorded and released by Gaye in 1966. The Doobies' version is, of course, much smoother with a fuller production. The original has a saxophone solo, and producer Ted Templeman suggested that 'Little Darling' would benefit from a similar addition. 'Jeff, however, had orchestrated a rather elaborate guitar interlude for him and Pat to play', Michael McDonald recalled. 'Jeff won that one – and to his credit, it was always a big moment in our live show that highlighted his and Pat's impressive abilities as guitarists.' 'Little Darling (I Need You)' was the first single from the *Livin' On The Front Line,* but barely cracked the top 50. It's accessible and competent, but inessential.

'You Belong To Me' (Simon, McDonald)

Featured on Best Of The Doobies Volume II (1981)

'You Belong To Me' is a co-composition by Michael McDonald and Carly Simon. 'I made a cassette recording of a chord progression I was playing around with', McDonald wrote. 'All I had was a roughly sketched-out melody – no lyrics except one four-word phrase, a placeholder serving only to point to where I thought the chorus could begin. Ted [Templeman] heard the tape and the phrase 'You belong to me' and instantly said, 'You should have Carly Simon write the lyrics to that.' I thought, 'If only.' So, Ted sent Carly the tape, and in no time, she sent back the original cassette and the beautiful lyrics she'd written in longhand and thus was born 'You Belong To Me' – without the two of us ever once sitting in the same room or even talking on the phone. She just took the vague melody I offered and sent back these well-crafted lyrics that instantly felt perfect the first time I sang them.'

'You Belong To Me' serves as a perfect lens into the Doobie Brothers' late-1970s transformation. Though not a major hit for the band, it showcases Michael McDonald's growing role as songwriter and vocalist; apart from some backing vocals, the arrangement and feel place it, almost, as a McDonald solo track. McDonald himself is in exquisite form, his phrasing precise and his vocal emotive without being melodramatic. The song's quiet intensity, coupled with its minor-key sophistication, embodies the album's ethos: smooth but not soft, emotional but never overwrought.

Carly Simon's version, released as a single to promote her 1978 album *Boys In The Trees*, was a huge hit in the US. The Doobies' take is a sleeper gem.

'Livin' On The Fault Line' (Simmons)

The album's title track is a compelling, polished, sophisticated mood piece – brooding, keyboard-driven and almost progressive in structure, but with a musically adventurous central section which leans into another new direction for The Doobie Brothers: funk/jazz. Pat Simmons' voice is hushed, navigating lyrics that speak to both geological instability (the San Andreas Fault runs through California) and metaphorical disarray. Jeff Baxter shines in a trademark solo. One can almost hear the tremor beneath the arrangement.

Simmons: 'I was always infatuated with San Francisco, its history and culture, so the lyrical content... is linked directly to the city. There are bunches of 1906 earthquake references in 'Fault Line', and I wanted to try something outside the pocket. Listening to the track even today, it's definitely outside! It's like five or six movements in one and more jazz-fusion than rock.'

'Nothin' But A Heartache' (McDonald)

Released as a single (with B-side 'Livin' On The Fault Line') in November 1977.
Charts: did not chart.

'Nothin' But A Heartache' was The Doobie Brothers' first miss since their debut – an alarming statistic for a band whose best of compilation from the year before was still in the charts. Despite its ambition, attempting a funk-rock fusion, the track feels slightly at odds with the album's polished soul textures. The horns, while energetic, sometimes overwhelm the arrangement, and the forced tempo contrasts with the smoother grooves elsewhere. Nevertheless, there is charm in its audacity: the track captures a snapshot of a band experimenting with funk while still grappling with the coherence of their evolving sound.

'Chinatown' (Simmons)
'Chinatown' is slow, jazzy and sly. Pat Simmons whispers his way through a tale that never quite resolves, but the arrangement is lovely – wistful guitar lines and Rhodes piano create an air of mystery. It's undeniably cinematic. "Chinatown' is one of my favourite tunes that I have ever been involved in writing', Pat Simmons confirms. 'The intricate arrangement, vocals and solos of 'Chinatown' are, to me, some of the coolest playing ever. Keith's drum part and Tiran's parts are inspired. Ted did some outstanding percussion that makes the whole track groove and percolate.' We should also give credit to Michael McDonald's vocal arrangements and Jeff Baxter's use of the guitar synthesiser.

'There's A Light' (McDonald)
Leaning into spiritual introspection, 'There's A Light' features gospel-inflected harmonies and soft, contemplative vocals. Thematically, it aligns with the album's introspective mood, offering a sense of searching and tentative hope rather than resolution. Norton Buffalo guests on harmonica.

'Need A Lady' (Porter)
Tiran Porter's 'Need A Lady' brings a sharp, soulful edge to the album. The song's confident grooves and smooth vocal lines reflect his R&B sensibilities, offering a sensual counterpoint to the more meditative tracks elsewhere. Its restrained arrangement allows Porter's delicious vocal performance to take centre stage.

'Larry The Logger Two-Step' (Simmons)
The album closes with Pat Simmons' ragtime-inspired guitar instrumental, a playful nod to Americana. Brisk, technically precise and entirely unexpected, the track demonstrates Simmons' versatility and willingness to inject levity and surprise into the album's conclusion. It is both a showcase of skill and a reminder of the Doobies' eclectic roots.

Minute By Minute (1978)

Personnel:
Patrick Simmons: vocals, guitars
Michael McDonald: vocals, piano, electric piano, organ, synthesisers
Jeff 'Skunk' Baxter: guitars
Tiran Porter: bass, vocals
John Hartman: drums, percussion
Keith Knudsen: drums, percussion, vocals
With:
Ted Templeman: drums, percussion
Bobby LaKind: congas, backing vocals
Tom Johnston: backing vocals
Nicolette Larson: vocals
Rosemary Butler: backing vocals
Norton Buffalo: harmonica
Herb Pedersen: banjo
Byron Berline: fiddle
Lester Abrams: electric piano
Bill Payne: synthesiser
Novi Novog: synthesiser
Sumner Mering: guitar
Andrew Love: saxophone
Ben Cauley: trumpet
Recorded at Warner Bros. Recording Studios, North Hollywood and Sunset Sound, Los Angeles, in 1978
Produced by Ted Templeman
Released 1 December 1978
Highest chart positions: US: 1, UK: did not chart

Livin' On The Fault Line would become the first Doobie Brothers album without a top 40 entry since their self-titled debut. Likewise, the second and third singles from *Takin' It To The Streets* hadn't set the charts alight. *Minute By Minute* wasn't quite a new band starting from scratch, but they needed a big hit to re-establish their commercial success. It had to be hard won. The album was released in mid-December 1978, too late for the Christmas market and at a traditional low point for record releases. Furthermore, *Rolling Stone* published a scathing review by Stephen Holden titled 'The Doobie Brothers dabble on and on':

> Ever since Michael McDonald joined the Doobie Brothers nearly four years ago, the group has skirted greatness without ever being able to mould its disparate sensibilities into a single, driving force. That's a shame, because singer/keyboardist McDonald (an ex-Steely Dan) is a major rock talent and the Doobies' only hope of becoming something more than a fading, middleweight, 'people's' boogie band.

> On *Take It To The Streets* and *Living On The Fault Line*, [Patrick] Simmons held his own as a writer and singer well enough so that he and McDonald appeared to complement each other. Not this time. *Minute By Minute*'s three predominantly Simmons-penned Cubano numbers ('Sweet Feelin'', 'You Never Change', 'Dependin' On You') are no better than second-rate lounge fare, while his 'Steamer Lane Breakdown' is a pleasant but trivial bit of streamlined bluegrass. 'Don't Stop To Watch The Wheels', a would-be full-tilt boogie, fails to tilt.
>
> Though there's no question that the new record's best songs are all primarily by Michael McDonald, even his work has suffered a slight loss. 'Open Your Eyes', a jittery post-Motown ballad written by McDonald with Lester Abrams and Patrick Henderson, is the LP's big winner.

Against this background, Warner Bros. extracted a single from the album in early 1979. 'What A Fool Believes' triggered The Doobie Brothers' most successful period, 1979 to 1982. In mid-April, *Minute By Minute* was at number one on the *Billboard* album charts and 'What A Fool Believes' was at the same position in the singles charts.

Within months of that negative review, The Doobie Brothers were on the cover of *Rolling Stone*.

By now, The Doobie Brothers had become – by most objective measures – Michael McDonald's band. His unmistakable voice, Fender Rhodes and sophisticated songwriting dominated the record. 'What A Fool Believes' would go on to define the era, win multiple Grammys and codify the sound some would later call 'yacht rock'. And yet, within this bold new incarnation of the band, Patrick Simmons remained a vital thread of continuity – a quiet but essential voice keeping the Doobie flame alive amid the satin-slick reinvention.

If McDonald brought the *future*, Simmons made sure the band didn't forget where it came from. He was the soul of the original band, folded carefully into a new body. His presence ensured that the Doobie Brothers' pivot into sophisticated soul-pop didn't feel like a cynical rebrand but rather an evolution. Without Simmons, *Minute By Minute* might have been a Michael McDonald solo album in all but name. Instead, it remains – thanks to Simmons' quiet stewardship – a Doobie Brothers album, albeit one in a tailored suit rather than denim.

Minute By Minute was nominated for Album of the Year at the 1980 Grammy Awards (losing to Billy Joel's *52nd Street*). The singles from the album won four Grammy awards: Record of the Year ('What A Fool Believes'), Song of the Year ('What A Fool Believes'), Best Arrangement Accompanying Vocals ('What A Fool Believes') and Best Pop Vocal Performance by a Duo, Group or Chorus ('Minute By Minute'). The album spent 87 weeks on the *Billboard* 200, topped the charts for several weeks and was certified triple-platinum.

Above: The 1973-1974 lineup. L-R: Keith Knudsen (drums, percussion), Tiran Porter (bass), Patrick Simmons (lead vocals, guitar, banjo), Tom Johnston (lead vocals, guitar, harmonica), John Hartman (drums, percussion). (*Alamy*)

Left: *The Doobie Brothers* (1971) – a tentative debut with flashes of identity, leaning heavily on blues and boogie while still feeling like a band in search of a direction. (*Warner Bros.*)

Right: *Toulouse Street* (1972) – The Doobies come into focus with a tighter sound and radio-friendly polish, adding a gospel-tinged energy that gave them their first real hits. (*Warner Bros.*)

Left: *The Captain And Me* (1973) – perhaps the best summary of the early Doobies, this is a confident, muscular record that blends hard-driving riffs with a greater sense of ambition. (*Warner Bros.*)

Right: *What Were Once Vices Are Now Habits* (1974) – darker, moodier and more eclectic, though it yielded their first number one with 'Black Water'. The experimentation hints at the band's broader musical horizons. (*Warner Bros.*)

Left: *Stampede* (1975) – ambitious in scope, pulling in strings, horns and a broader palette of styles, sometimes to its credit, sometimes not. A fascinating, slightly overstuffed bridge between eras. (*Warner Bros.*)

Right: *Takin' It To The Streets* (1976) – Michael McDonald's arrival changes everything, introducing a more soulful, keyboard-driven sound. It's a brave reinvention that largely works, even if it alienated some long-time fans. (*Warner Bros.*)

Above: The original lineup in 1970. L-R: John Hartman, Tom Johnston, Dave Shogren and Pat Simmons. (*Michael Ochs Archives/Getty Images*)

Below: The lineup that recorded *Toulouse Street* (1972), *The Captain And Me* (1973) and *What Were Once Vices Are Now Habits* (1974). L-R: Patrick Simmons, Tom Johnston, Michael Hossack, John Hartman and Tiran Porter. (*Alamy*)

Above: In concert in 1976 with Jeff Baxter (far right) and members of the Memphis Horns. (*Barry Schultz*)

Below: The Doobie Brothers on the Dutch TV show *TopPop* in 1974. (*Alamy*)

Above: In London, January 1974. L-R: John Hartman, Tom Johnston, Tiran Porter, Patrick Simmons and Keith Knudsen. (*Michael Ochs Archives/Getty Images*)

Below: The Doobie Brothers in Holland in 1975. (*Van Houten*)

Above: The transitional lineup, circa 1976, with both Tom Johnston and Michael McDonald. (*Michael Ochs Archives/Getty Images*)

Below: Pat, Tiran and Skunk at the Reading Festival, 1977. (*Alamy*)

Left: *Best Of The Doobies* (1976) is a concise and impeccably sequenced collection that cemented their reputation, distilling the early years into a radio-friendly canon. (*Warner Bros.*)

Right: *Livin' On The Fault Line* (1977) – perhaps their most subdued effort, leaning toward introspection and atmosphere. Admirably subtle, though occasionally in danger of disappearing into the background. (*Warner Bros.*)

Left: *Minute By Minute* (1978) – the commercial peak, sleekly produced and Grammy-anointed, with 'What A Fool Believes' as its centrepiece. (*Warner Bros.*)

Right: *One Step Closer* (1980) – the last of the McDonald era, professional and smooth but lacking the urgency of earlier work. The sound of a great band easing toward a pause. (*Warner Bros.*)

Left: Five years after the first volume, *Best Of The Doobies, Volume II* (1981) covered the later McDonald-led era, being smoother, more urbane and less guitar-driven than its predecessor. (*Warner Bros.*)

Right: 1983's *Farewell Tour* drew a close to the band. For now. (*Warner Bros.*)

Above: The band performing at the Oakland Coliseum on 30 December 1978. Bobby LaKind plays percussion (top right). (*Ed Perlstein*)

Left: (L-R, top row) Cornelius Bumpus, Patrick Simmons, Keith Knudsen, (L-R, bottom row) John McFee, Tiran Porter, Michael McDonald and Chet McCracken outside a Benton's Barber Shop in 1979. (*Michael Ochs Archives/Getty Images*)

Right and below: The Doobie Brothers attended the Grammys in 1980, where they won four awards. (*Michael Ochs Archives/ Getty Images*)

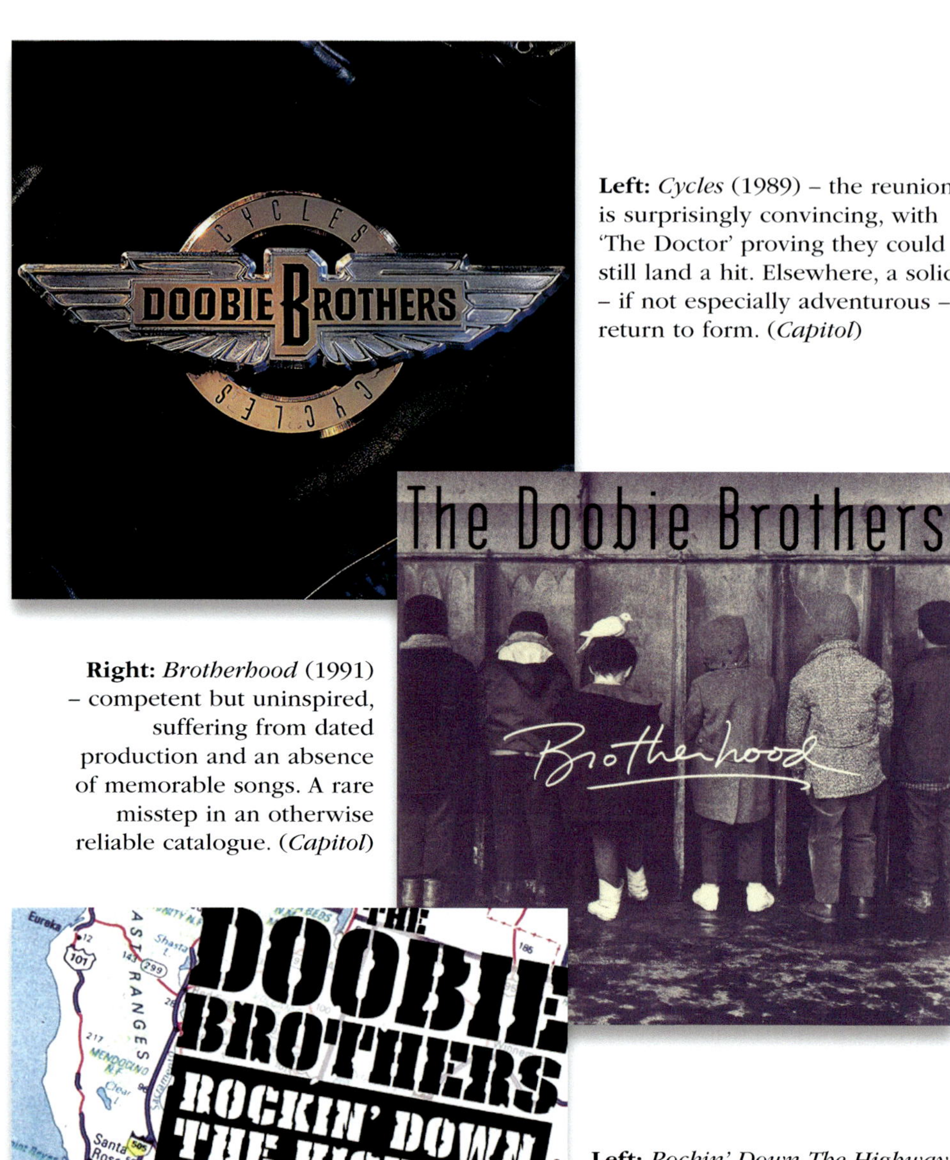

Left: *Cycles* (1989) – the reunion is surprisingly convincing, with 'The Doctor' proving they could still land a hit. Elsewhere, a solid – if not especially adventurous – return to form. (*Capitol*)

Right: *Brotherhood* (1991) – competent but uninspired, suffering from dated production and an absence of memorable songs. A rare misstep in an otherwise reliable catalogue. (*Capitol*)

Left: *Rockin' Down The Highway: The Wildlife Concert* (1996) – a strong reunion set, reminding audiences of the breadth of the catalogue. The performances feel fresh, proving the Doobies had lost little of their power. (*Sony*)

Right: *Long Train Runnin' 1970-2000* (1999) – a sprawling four-disc retrospective that traces every twist of the Doobies' long career, from biker-bar boogie to McDonald's sleek soul and beyond. (*Rhino*)

Left: *Sibling Rivalry* (2000) – a late-career outing that mixes new ideas with echoes of the past. Not essential, but a respectable reminder of their craft. (*Pyramid/Rhino*)

Right: *Greatest Hits* (2001) presents The Doobies not as a group that changed course midstream, but as one that evolved with curiosity and conviction, even at the cost of coherence. (*Warner Bros./Rhino*)

Left: *Live At Wolf Trap* (2004) – a confident and well-recorded show, capturing the band in fine late-career form. Familiar hits are delivered with energy rather than nostalgia. (*Sanctuary*)

Right: *World Gone Crazy* (2010) – polished and varied, with guest spots adding some colour, though its strongest moments remain rooted in the band's classic sound. A welcome, if modest, return. (*DooBro*)

Left: *Southbound* (2014) – Doobie classics reimagined with country artists, producing mixed results: some inspired, others less so. It's more of a celebration than an artistic statement. (*Arista Nashville*)

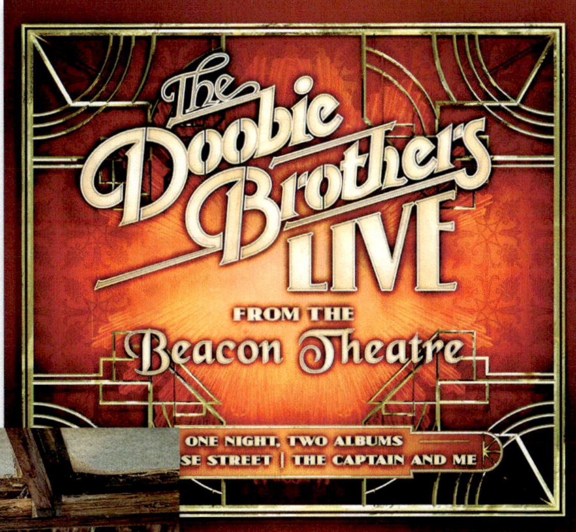

Right: *Live From The Beacon Theatre* (2019) presents live performances of *Toulouse Street* and *The Captain And Me* in their entirety. (*Rhino*)

Left: *Liberté* (2021) – confident and contemporary, showing the band are still capable of strong writing and tight playing. A surprisingly vital addition rather than a mere footnote. (*DB Entertainment/Island*)

Right: *Walk This Road* (2025) – the first album of new material with McDonald in decades: a blend of classic soul-rock and veteran craftsmanship. Expectations were high, and not without reason. (*Warner Bros./Rhino*)

Above: Back on the road in 1995, with new bassist Skylark, a re-recruited Michael McDonald and guest guitarist Bernie Chiaravalle, who temporarily substituted for the unavailable John McFee. (*Getty*)

Below: Pat, Tom and John – still rockin' down the highway.

'Here To Love You' (McDonald)
Released as a single (with B-side 'Wynken, Blynken And Nod') in 1982. Charts: US: 65.
Featured on Best Of The Doobies Volume II (1981)
The album opens not with a bang, but a smooth shimmer. McDonald's piano leads a low-slung groove, punctuated by percussion, saxophone, fat bass and gospel-tinged backing vocals. It's a mission statement: grown-up, laid-back, emotionally assured. As usual, McDonald's vocals are outstanding. He may not offer anything very new here, but the professionalism and musicality practically shimmers. 'Here To Love You' was released as a single in 1982 to promote the band's second 'best of' collection, reaching number 65.

'What A Fool Believes' (McDonald, Loggins)
Released as a single (with B-side 'Don't Stop To Watch The Wheels') in January 1979. Charts: US: 1, UK: 31.
Featured on Best Of The Doobies Volume II (1981)
'What A Fool Believes' is sophisticated pop at its apex. The genius lies in its tension: syncopated keyboards, lyrical ambiguity and a melody that floats rather than drives. Michael McDonald delivers one of his finest performances – wistful, restrained and devastating.

"What A Fool Believes'… was not a fast or easy delivery', McDonald wrote. 'I started with nothing but that verse piano riff… along with some words I jotted down on the back of an envelope on a flight from New York back to LA: 'She came from somewhere back in his long ago'. At that point, I was just poking at the idea of how two people could look back on the same event with two completely different perspectives. That's all I had. I played that rough, still-unfinished sketch of the song idea for Ted Templeman in his office one day, and his immediate response was 'That's a hit!' And to his everlasting credit, he stayed on me about it for weeks and months. 'I'm tellin' ya, you gotta finish that one!' And each time, I reassured him I would. But alas, it stayed unfinished for the longest time. Months later, Tiran Porter told me he happened to run into Kenny Loggins, whom I had never met but long admired. Kenny was writing some of the more musically sophisticated songs out there. And now, to my surprise and good fortune, Kenny expressed an interest in writing with me and gave Tiran his number to pass along. I was beyond excited. Kenny and I made an appointment to get together at my house to write, and when the day arrived, I was anxiously at it early, reviewing some unfinished song ideas, looking through books of lyrics for possible titles… anything. You never know what long-discarded scrap of an idea might be just the spark you're looking for. I remembered that syncopated piano motif and found the envelope with what few lyrics I had.'

McDonald played the half-written song through on his piano. 'At that exact moment, the doorbell rang, and I opened the door to find Kenny Loggins, struggling with his guitar… the first words out of his mouth: 'What was that you were just playing? Is that something new?' I readily assured Kenny that it was as yet totally unfinished and something I wondered if we might work on together. His response: 'Perfect, let's jump into that one first.' I already had the opening bit: 'She came from somewhere back in his long ago/Sentimental fool don't see/Trying hard to recreate what had yet to be created', And Kenny, just from hearing that much on the other side of the door, had already come up with the next melodic bit, which soon became: 'She ... had a place in his life/ He ... never made her think twice'. Kenny is one of the best songwriters I've ever worked with. The strength of his melodies would often dictate the chord progression, even without an instrument, which greatly impressed me… we found that lift into the chorus: 'What a fool believes… he sees…' Over the course of two days, we finished our first song together. Piece of cake.'

The Doobies' recording was edited together from several different takes in pursuit of the perfect performance. It includes Bill Payne playing synthesiser and drums by Keith Knudsen and Ted Templeman. Templeman, however, was never convinced by the song. 'I heard nothing in that song', he said in Johnston's and Simmons' joint memoirs. 'To me, it was a mess… it just went all over the place looking for some kind of direction, but never found it. To be honest, I still don't hear it today.'

Despite its producer's reservations, 'What A Fool Believes' would become The Doobies' second number one, for a single week in April 1979. An extended 12" disco remix is also available with additional percussion by the prolific session musician Jimmy Maelen.

Kenny Loggins released the first version of 'What A Fool Believes' on his album *Nightwatch* (July 1978), six months before The Doobie Brothers. Loggins' vocal delivery is warmer, more laid-back and has a singer-songwriter softness in contrast to the urgency and emotional punch of Michael McDonald's. The leaner, more acoustic-driven arrangement from *Nightwatch* contrasts with the hit single's tighter, funk-inflected groove. The Doobies' brighter tempo and punchier attack – with a 'radio hit' energy – makes Loggins' more understated version less memorable, however. They both have their place, but The Doobies take the trophy.

'Minute By Minute' (McDonald, Abrams)

Released as a single (with B-side 'Sweet Feelin'') in April 1979. Charts: US: 14. UK: 47.

Featured on Best Of The Doobies Volume II (1981)

'Minute By Minute' was co-written by Michael McDonald with singer, songwriter, musician and producer Lester Abrams. 'When we wrote the song,' McDonald wrote, 'I had in mind a certain kind of hypnotic feel; I don't want to say 'precise' but a very distinct clocklike 6/8 meter that I didn't know how to quite articulate. Kind of a jazz shuffle, but with very little swing, if you will. Sort of a gospel syncopation to it, but… Like I said, I didn't know how to explain it.'

The basic track was cut by McDonald on piano with drummer Keith Knudsen. 'I stayed put at my Fender Rhodes,' McDonald noted, 'and Keith hung in there on drums till we achieved that elusive, linear groove as best we could. I think I browbeat poor Keith to death to get the track we used. And he probably played it right every time; I was just so locked in and neurotic about wanting the song to have no noticeable swing.'

'Minute By Minute' is a slow burner – sparse, steady and quietly intense. McDonald's voice is all breathy sensuality, supported by delicate harmonies, velvety-smooth piano and a tick-tock rhythm section that reflects the lyrical theme of hanging on, moment to moment. There's no climax here, only a smouldering groove that holds its line with graceful resolve. It's magnificent.

'Dependin' On You' (McDonald, Simmons)

Released as a single (with B-side 'How Do the Fools Survive?') in July 1979.
Charts: US: 25.
Featured on Best Of The Doobies Volume II (1981)

It's notable that the first four songs on *Minute By Minute* were (co-)written by Michael McDonald and that, in due course, all of these were released as singles. 'Dependin' On You' is an authentic blend of the Doobies' old and new sound, written, appropriately enough, by McDonald and Simmons in McDonald's small home studio. It's the most Doobie-like track on the album in the classic sense – brighter tempo, more prominent guitars (yes, a solo!) and a vocal that hearkens back to 'South City Midnight Lady'. It's charming, catchy and slightly unkempt, which makes it all the more refreshing amid the rest of the album's smoothness. Backing vocals are enriched by Nicolette Larson and Rosemary Butler. It might not be *the* signature hit of *Minute By Minute*, but it's integral in completing the album's narrative – one that embraces soulful polish without losing its rock edge.

'Don't Stop To Watch The Wheels' (Simmons, Baxter, Ebert)

The groove is built on an insistent funk pulse: competent and slick, but lacking the emotional weight of the tracks surrounding it. Jeff Baxter's guitar flourishes add welcome colour to a rockier, rhythm-forward feel, even if the delivery is much politer than, say, 'Without You' or 'China Grove'. Tom Johnston guests on backing vocals while Norton Buffalo plays harmonica, giving the song the distinctive texture of the band's earlier albums. It provides balance against the smooth, soul-infused direction brought by Michael McDonald elsewhere on the album and is a compelling example both of the Doobie Brothers' stylistic versatility and of the transitional dynamics at play during a pivotal era in their career.

'Open Your Eyes' (McDonald, Abrams, Henderson)

Michael McDonald delivers another introspective performance over a swampy groove. The chord progressions hint at gospel, and the mood is contemplative. It's an album track in the best sense – measured, moody and emotionally lived-in. It provides a reflective shift in the album's narrative whilst (almost) asking you to tap your foot. An underrated deep cut, worth revisiting.

'Sweet Feelin'' (Simmons, Templeman)
Pure mid-1970s West Coast, it could come straight from Crosby, Stills & Nash's 1977 reunion album, or classic-era Little River Band. It offers a breezy, soft-rock moment with a gentle, soulful edge that contrasts the album's more polished soul-laden tracks. Nicolette Larson is prominently featured on vocals, adding warmth and sweetness to the performance.

'Steamer Lane Breakdown' (Simmons)
Pat Simmons once again reminds us that the Doobies didn't start as a soul-pop outfit. This electric bluegrass instrumental is brisk and delightfully out of step with the rest of the record. A hoedown in the middle of a Doobie Brothers album? Only Simmons could pull it off without wrecking the flow.

'You Never Change' (Simmons)
What sounds like a Michael McDonald song was written by Pat Simmons: both men sing the track together – low-key, yearning, exquisitely arranged. The chord progressions are pure adult contemporary jazz-pop, smooth, sophisticated and controlled, giving the track a grown-up, cosmopolitan vibe without ever getting heavy or challenging.

The lyric feels like an epilogue to 'What A Fool Believes'. That song is about nostalgia, lost possibilities and misremembered romance ... the idea of chasing something that was never really there. 'You Never Change' picks up on that reflective tone but shifts the perspective: instead of looking back at a fleeting fantasy, it observes the constancy of a person. There's a sense of acceptance, almost resignation, that feels like an afterword to the earlier story. It's not quite as gripping as the big hit, but it reinforces the thematic unity of the album: love lost, time passed, lessons learned (or not).

'How Do The Fools Survive?' (McDonald, Bayer Sager)
The album closes on an unexpectedly epic note. Co-written by Michael McDonald and Carole Bayer Sager, this five-minute track gradually swells to a long instrumental passage with a trademark one-take Jeff Baxter guitar solo. Despite its tempo, the song has a melancholic feel, blending soft rock, soul and pop-jazz elements. Its lyrical content is oblique but reflects struggle and perseverance, consistent with McDonald's reflective approach to songwriting during this period.

Positioned as the final track on *Minute By Minute*, 'How Do The Fools Survive?' provides a powerful endnote to an album otherwise characterised by groove-driven songs like 'What A Fool Believes' and 'Dependin' On You'.

One Step Closer (1980)

Personnel:
Patrick Simmons: vocals, guitars
John McFee: guitars, backing vocals
Michael McDonald: vocals, keyboards
Cornelius Bumpus: saxophone, organ, vocals
Tiran Porter: bass
Keith Knudsen: drums, backing vocals
Chet McCracken: drums, vibraphone, marimbas
With:
Bobby LaKind: congas, bongos, backing vocals
Nicolette Larson: backing vocals
Patrick Henderson: keyboards
Lee Thornburg: trumpet, flugelhorn
Chris Thompson: backing vocals
Ted Templeman: tambourine, cowbell, maracas, backing vocals
Jerome Jumonville: tenor saxophone
Joel Peskin: baritone saxophone
Bill Armstrong: trumpet
Recorded at Sunset Sound Recorders, Hollywood, Warner Bros. Recording Studios, North Hollywood, United Sound Recorders, Detroit and A&R Recorders, New York, in 1980
Produced by Ted Templeman
Released 17 September 1980
Highest chart positions: US: 3, UK: 53

The Doobie Brothers almost broke up in January/February 1979 after a run of live dates in Japan. With discord in the ranks, principally between Jeff Baxter and Michael McDonald, a band discussion led to a tough decision. '[Baxter] was very entertaining and had amazing chops', Pat Simmons noted. 'But he had a big personality that was sometimes over the top and could eventually start getting to people.'

According to McDonald, 'Suddenly everybody realised that, with things as they were, it wasn't fulfilling. People felt like they were just floating, and it was just a matter of realising what was best for whom. Was it best for me to quit and have a solo career? I wanted to do a solo record, but I didn't want to quit the Doobies; I never wanted to perform on my own. Or, was it best for Jeff to quit and produce other acts the way he wanted to? The band wanted to be more structured, hard-hitting and direct, and Jeff really wanted to do a more jazzy, avant-garde kind of a soloist band, which is his forte. So basically, we were forced with a decision, and we had to be honest with each other. Was it better for 30 guys to be out of work if I quit and tried to re-form the band from a writer's standpoint, or was it better for Jeff to pursue the things he wanted to do?'

'We had a meeting in the hotel', drummer Keith Knudsen told Mark Bego in 1980. 'Everybody had a good cry; we all cried. It was hard to let go. After the tour, Pat and Mike went to Hawaii. I followed, and while Pat went on to Tahiti, Mike and I relaxed in Maui and watched the whales for about ten days. We didn't talk about the break-up too much.'

'We all left Japan on different flights,' Michael McDonald noted, 'without much real communication between us. Keith and John had their issues, Jeff Baxter and I were butting heads more frequently, and even Pat, I sensed, was starting to be increasingly demoralised with the overall direction of the organisation; it was growing further and further away from its original roots. Three of the members wanted John Hartman's head and thought he should be fired, and the other two felt that was a little harsh and unfair, as John was one of the founding members of the band. In the end, the only unanimous agreement we could come to was: 'Fuck it! That's it. We're done!' So we decided to officially break up.'

Knudsen: 'But when we got back to LA, Tiran, Pat, Mike and I decided to stay together. 'After a couple of months as a four-piece, during which time both 'What A Fool Believes' and *Minute By Minute* were number one hits, three new members signed up. John McFee was formerly of Clover with Huey Lewis.

'Clover had moved back from England', McFee told *Coachella Valley Weekly* in 2019. 'Our British record contract had expired, and our managers were going through a somewhat contentious splitting up of their management company. They were having some serious disagreements about who would continue managing which of their artists, and we were caught in a legal limbo where we couldn't book shows and couldn't record, or basically do anything having to do with moving forward with our career. This was also right as my son was born, and I felt an increased level of responsibility in my life, so I started taking work to generate income – I did some touring with Carlene Carter, started gigging with my good friend Norton Buffalo as part of his band and things like that. All the time, I was hoping for some solution to the situation with Clover so that we could start doing things again, as I still believed in what we were trying to do and considered the band to be my family. One day, my wife was speaking with Keith Knudsen's wife about things, and Keith's wife mentioned that the Doobies were looking for a replacement for Jeff and that Keith had thought of asking me, but that because I had turned down some other high-profile gig offers because of my commitment to Clover, he hadn't done so. My wife told her that the current circumstances were perhaps different and that maybe he should speak with me, so Keith talked to me about it, and I ended up going down with him to the Doobies rehearsal house on the coast south of San Francisco to feel things out. I played a number of songs with the band, and they said I was in if I wanted to be, and that was how it all started.' 'We had met John at Reading Festival [in 1977]', Tom Johnston recalled. 'John came to the show.'

McFee was also familiar to Ted Templeman: McFee had played pedal steel guitar on two albums that Templeman had produced for Van Morrison, *Tupelo Honey* (1971) and *St. Dominic's Preview* (1972). He impressed Pat Simmons by finger picking 'Slack Key Soquel Rag' at his audition. 'John can really play anything, from jazz to fusion to pop to rock 'n' roll', said Pat Simmons. 'He's just one of the most versatile players you will ever meet. Electric, acoustic, pedal steel; he's just incredible. He also had a really cool look and was overall just a great person. He would be the perfect addition to the Doobie Brothers.'

Session drummer Chester 'Chet' McCraken was recommended by Michael McDonald. McCraken had played on albums by America (*Hat Trick*, 1973), Helen Reddy (*Reddy*, 1979), Hank Williams Jr (*Family Tradition*, 1979) and many others. He was familiar with 'China Grove' and 'Listen To The Music' from playing the songs with various bar bands. 'I loved the group's early hits', he told author Mark Bego when he joined the band. 'It was the perfect kind of music for its time. I was doing well as a session percussionist. I stopped worrying about making the house payments about three years ago. But playing with the Doobies is an honour... and it sure beats working on Radio Shack commercials! Emotionally, it was like stepping on a rocket ship and trying to hold on!'

A seventh member, saxophonist and keyboard player Cornelius Bumpus, was formerly of the band Original Haze, who supported The Doobie Brothers in 1976. He also played in a reformed Moby Grape. 'I ran into him all the time in Santa Cruz', Pat Simmons said. 'He would stand out there downtown on Santa Cruz Avenue with his sax case open, just blowing his sweet sounds, and people would be dropping money in the case. I would stand there listening, thinking, holy shit – this guy is great! Cornelius told me on a good day, he could make maybe 30 or 40 bucks playing in the streets. And with us, he would start out making about $5000 a week. A big step up for him, but he certainly deserved it.'

During 1979, the new lineup completed a 40-city US tour, which included two appearances at Madison Square Garden (19 and 20 September) as part of a series of five concerts organised by the Musicians United for Safe Energy (MUSE). Highlights of the concerts were released on a triple live album, *No Nukes*, in December 1979, the first official live recordings by The Doobie Brothers. The tracks included are 'Dependin' On You', 'Lotta Love' (with Nicolette Larson), 'Power' (with John Hall) and 'Takin' It To The Streets' (with many of the cast of the concerts and a shared lead vocal by James Taylor). They also appear in the following year's film performing 'Dependin' On You', 'What A Fool Believes' and 'Takin' It To The Streets'. Most of their set is available online, if you know where to look.

At the start of a new decade, however, there was just the matter of a follow-up to their most successful album. *One Step Closer*, the band's ninth studio album, is the sound of a group caught in a paradox: still professional, still proficient, but beginning to drift apart. The gloss is thicker, the edges softer and the cohesion – so striking on *Minute By Minute* – is beginning to dissolve. What remains is an album that's more *refined* than *inspired*, more *competent* than *compelling*. The album went platinum, but one could argue that it was purely on the band's reputation and the strength of the single 'Real Love', the band's fourth and last top ten hit. It's certainly very polished, but one misses the raw energy of 'China Grove' or even 'Taking It To The Streets'. The songs are professionally constructed, the arrangements pristine – but the vitality, the playfulness, the *bandness* of the Doobies is fading. Pat Simmons offers moments of continuity, but seems half-in, half-out. The rest of the band contribute like seasoned session men, which, of course, some of them were. 'For me, *One Step Closer* was one of the most fun projects we'd done since *Takin' It To The Streets*', Michael McDonald noted. 'I didn't realise then that it would be the last studio album I'd record with the Doobies for 34 years.'

A few weeks after the album's release, long-time bassist Tiran Porter left The Doobie Brothers. He had reportedly grown frustrated with the band's increasing reliance on studio polish and the softening of their musical direction. He's the only band member not to have a (co-)writing credit on *One Step Closer*.

Porter departed amicably, but clearly at odds with the band's shift away from its rock-and-funk roots toward polished, adult-oriented soul-pop. He was replaced in the touring band by seasoned session player Willie Weeks, who had toured with McDonald in Randy Newman's live band, as well as playing with George Harrison, David Bowie, Stevie Wonder and others. Weeks' bass solo on the live version of 'Voices Inside (Everything Is Everything)' from *Donny Hathaway Live* (1972) is legendary and widely cited by fellow musicians.

'Dedicate This Heart' (McDonald, Anka)

'Dedicate This Heart' is a crisp, punchy opener that sets the tone: synth-heavy, funk-tinged and built around a typically elegant McDonald melody. The lyrics are by 'My Way' co-composer Paul Anka. The horn arrangement is tasteful, the rhythm section airtight. And yet, for all its polish, it never quite takes flight. One misses the sense of urgency that opened earlier albums. It's slick and serviceable, but hardly arresting. Dionne Warwick's version from her 1981 album *Hot! Live And Otherwise* is a much better prospect.

'Real Love' (McDonald, Henderson)

Released as a single (with B-side: 'Thank You Love') in August 1980. Charts: US: 5. Featured on Best Of The Doobies Volume II (1981)

'Real Love' was released as a single a few weeks ahead of the album: the first new music from The Doobie Brothers for almost two years. It was the band's fourth top ten hit and the first to feature neither Tom Johnston nor Patrick Simmons as composers on either side of the 7" single. The co-writer here, Patrick Henderson, was a gospel keyboard player, songwriter and producer friend of Michael McDonald.

It originates in plans for a Michael McDonald solo album. 'Personally, I wasn't viewing the solo record as any kind of jumping-off point or new career direction', he wrote in his memoirs. 'The Doobies were still my first priority… [but] before we started work on the Doobies' next album, I went in and recorded the first couple of tracks for my album, one of which was a song… called 'Real Love', an upbeat but lyrically mournful resignation as far as love is concerned. I felt it was the best song I had at the time and would have been a terrific addition to my solo album. But my allegiance to the band was such that I believed I owed my best effort to them first.'

'Real Love' captures the full McDonald aesthetic: layered keyboards, mid-tempo restraint and emotionally ambivalent lyrics sung with velvet gravitas. It's meticulously produced, melodically rich and utterly of its time.

'No Stoppin' Us Now' (Simmons, McDonald, Thompson)
Upbeat and horn-driven, 'No Stoppin' Us Now' sounds like a refugee from an entirely different album. It tries valiantly to inject energy into the track list – and Simmons sings with genuine gusto – but the songwriting is pedestrian despite co-credits to Simmons, Michael McDonald and Chris Thompson of Manfred Mann's Earth Band (who adds backing vocals). It feels like an attempt to balance McDonald's introspective cool with some good-time swagger, but the parts don't quite cohere. The guitar solo feels dropped in from another song entirely.

'Thank You Love' (Bumpus)
Cornelius Bumpus writes and sings some Latin jazz, which is the very definition of the West Coast sound of 1980 (pejoratively called yacht rock in some quarters). There is a vibraphone solo. At 6.22, it's one of the longest songs in the band's extensive back catalogue. It sits well on *One Step Closer*, but fans wanting some guitar-based bite might well skip this track.

'One Step Closer' (Knudsen, Carter, McFee)
Released as a single (with B-side 'South Bay Strut') in November 1980. Charts: US: 24.
Featured on Best Of The Doobies Volume II (1981)
The album's title track is an ensemble piece, co-written by Keith Knudsen with John McFee and Carlene Carter and sung by Knudsen, McDonald and Bumpus. Its shuffle rhythm and vocal harmonies offer a rare moment of unity – a throwback to the *Toulouse Street* era (on which none of the writers were involved), albeit dressed in 1980s studio finery. It's breezy and likeable, if not especially deep.

'Keep This Train A-Rollin' (McDonald)
Released as a single (with B-side 'Just In Time') in January 1981. Charts: US: 62.
Another train metaphor. The groove is swampy, the vibe almost Little Feat-esque (it starts like that band's 'Spanish Moon'), with skipping piano, organ,

steel guitar flourishes and a more organic 1970s feel than most of the album. It's a welcome shift in texture, even if it doesn't fully ignite.

'Just In Time' (Simmons)
This taut funk from Pat Simmons, co-sung by Nicolette Larson, checks out after two-and-a-half minutes. It fits seamlessly into the album's flow: smooth and likeable if not particularly memorable.

'South Bay Strut' (McCracken, McFee)
An instrumental from new boys Chet McCracken and John McFee finds the band in jazz-fusion-lite territory. It's polished, with flashes of musicality, but ultimately comes off as filler. It's the sort of track that would make fine background music for a yacht club brunch. Technically proficient, emotionally neutral. It was nominated for Best Pop Instrumental Performance at the 23rd Annual Grammy Awards, losing out to 'One On One' by Bob James & Earl Klugh.

'One By One' (LaKind, McDonald)
Featured on Best Of The Doobies Volume II (1981)
The album closes with a Simmons-McDonald duet that typifies the record as a whole: lush, low-key and emotionally sealed off. There's craft here. With his natural ear for harmony and deceptively intricate compositions, Michael McDonald could write chord progressions in his sleep that others would kill for. But the spark is missing.

As a closer, it leaves the album in a kind of suspended melancholy, appropriate perhaps, given the band's impending fragmentation.

Related Releases

'Can't Let It Get Away' (Simmons, McFee, Larson)
Released in Japan and Australia in 1981
This is one of a series of records given away as a 'Freebie' in 1981 in a Coca-Cola competition in Japan. It was also released as a single in Australia and, unlisted, on the Australian pressing of *Best Of The Doobies Volume II*. It's a limp rock song sung by Pat Simmons, recorded for the incomplete album which was due to come after *One Step Closer*. It's one of only two available tracks that were recorded in these sessions (the other, 'Olana', is on the *Long Train Runnin'* box set). 'Can't Let It Get Away' is the most difficult Doobie Brothers song to track down, as it's never been re-released digitally. It can be heard on YouTube, and there is a promo video that is available to view.

Best Of The Doobies Volume II (1981)
Track listing: 'Little Darling (I Need You)', 'Echoes Of Love', 'You Belong To Me', 'One Step Closer', 'What A Fool Believes', 'Dependin' On You', 'Here To Love You', 'One By One', 'Real Love', 'Minute By Minute'

This compilation album, released in November 1981, includes ten songs from the Doobies' previous three albums. Five of these had been big hits, including their second number one and arguably their best-known song, 'What A Fool Believes'. 'Here To Love You', originally from *Minute By Minute*, would be issued as a single to promote *Best Of The Doobies II* in early 1982 (US: 65). This is remixed and with an instrumental section removed, reducing the running time by 30 seconds. The B-side was a version of 'Wynken, Blynken And Nod', first released as the opening track on the compilation album *In Harmony: A Sesame Street Record* in October 1980 alongside kids' songs by the likes of Warner Bros artists James Taylor, Carly Simon, Bette Midler, Al Jarreau, Linda Ronstadt, Dr. John and George Benson.

Although no-one could have predicted it, four months after the release of this record, The Doobie Brothers were no longer a functioning band, at least not in any creatively cohesive sense. Patrick Simmons had departed, Michael McDonald was poised for a solo career and the group were quietly winding down. Unintentionally, *Best Of The Doobies Volume II* served as a sort of musical postscript to the band's second act. Where *Best Of The Doobies (*1976) had encapsulated the rugged, denim-clad exuberance of the early years – Tom Johnston's raspy vocals, Simmons' acoustic textures and the twin-guitar California drive – *Volume II* instead chronicles a period defined by Rhodes pianos, jazzy chord extensions and adult contemporary introspection. It is, in essence, a different band with Michael McDonald featuring prominently throughout. This makes this compilation a polarising affair. For fans of the early, guitar-centric Doobies, *Volume II* is a sleek, air-conditioned detour into another universe. For those who embraced the band's transformation into Grammy-winning architects of blue-eyed soul, this is a well-sequenced portrait of the band's refined late-period sound. Most notably, there is almost no Pat Simmons. His presence is reduced to 'Dependin' On You', 'Echoes Of Love' and 'One Step Closer', the latter a track that, while pleasant, is hardly essential. This editorial choice makes *Volume II* feel like a curated summary of the band's Michael McDonald years, with only token gestures toward their broader musical DNA. It's not inaccurate, but it is incomplete. The band photograph on the reverse of the album shows an eight-piece lineup with Bobby LaKind and Willie Weeks listed as official members.

Tom Johnston released his second solo album, *Still Feels Good*, in 1981. It includes contributions from Pat Simmons and Bobby LaKind. 1982 saw the release of an album called *That Was Then, The Early Recordings Of Michael McDonald*. This collects McDonald's early 1970s singles produced by Rick Jarrard for Bell, most of them original compositions. A very dodgy Russian CD extends this to 16 tracks with the inclusion of hard-to-find singles by The Delrays ('Always Something There To Remind Me') and 'Mike' McDonald ('God Knows' b/w 'If You Won't I Will' and 'Where Do I Go From Here' b/w 'Can You Feel It?').

Farewell Tour (1983)

Personnel:
Patrick Simmons: vocals, guitars
John McFee: guitars, pedal steel guitar, violin, backing vocals
Michael McDonald: keyboards, synthesisers, lead and backing vocals
Cornelius Bumpus: saxophones, Hammond organ, synthesisers, vocals
Keith Knudsen: drums, tambourine, vocals
Chet McCracken: drums, vibraphone, tambourine, timbales
Willie Weeks: bass, backing vocals
Bobby LaKind: congas, bongos, percussion, backing vocals
With:
Tom Johnston: vocals, guitar
Joe Crowley: harmonica
Recorded on 3 September 1982 at Irvine Meadows Amphitheatre, Irvine, California; 4 September 1982 at Universal Amphitheatre, Universal City, California; 10-11 September 1982 at Hearst Greek Theatre, Berkeley, California
Produced by Ted Templeman
Released: June 1983
Highest chart positions: US: 3, UK: 53
Track listing: 'Slippery St. Paul' (excerpt from The Doobie Brothers, 1971), 'Takin' It To The Streets', 'Jesus Is Just Alright', 'Minute By Minute', 'Can't Let It Get Away', 'Listen To The Music', 'Echoes Of Love', 'What A Fool Believes', 'Black Water', 'You Belong To Me' (released as a single with B-side 'South City Midnight Lady'. US: 79), 'Slack Key Soquel Rag', 'Steamer Lane Breakdown', 'South City Midnight Lady', 'Olana', 'Don't Start Me Talkin'', 'Long Train Runnin'', 'China Grove'

By March 1982, Pat Simmons had decided to leave The Doobie Brothers. He was, by then, the last remaining founder member. His hand was forced when the band's management wanted to move the base of the band's operations to Los Angeles. 'I didn't want to live in Los Angeles', Simmons said in his memoirs. 'I also didn't appreciate the lack of respect. Forcing my hand and costing me money to further the career of our manager didn't seem right. Then a big storm up north hit, and I had a lot of work to do at my house; we had no power for more than a week, and there was tons of damage in Santa Cruz. It was time for the band to rehearse, and I couldn't get out. But we did have commitments, so it was hard. Everybody became somewhat uncompromising. They all went down to L. A. to rehearse. I felt disrespected, and I knew this was basically it. I called Mike on the phone and said, 'The Doobie Brothers, for me, are not a Southern California band. We are a Northern California band. We're a San Jose band. I think I might be done with all of this."

The Doobie Brothers performed one show in New York that spring without Simmons, then returned to California to assemble for rehearsals. Michael

McDonald: 'I guess the thinking was that we might still, at some point, tour. But from the first song we played down, the elephant in the room loomed large: the lack of any original members at all. Those of us who remained just didn't seem to add up to the Doobie Brothers anymore. It was a solemn moment that none of us wanted to face… it seemed we all had come in that day thinking the same thing. I was just the one who didn't have the sense to not bring it up. I couldn't tell if some of the guys were mad at me for broaching the subject, and I'd have understood if they felt like I was trying to make some unilateral decision for everyone. But I wasn't. I was just trying to articulate what I saw as the truth in that moment: that I didn't feel any more prepared than anyone else on that stage to step up to fill Pat's shoes as the leader of the Doobie Brothers.'

Simmons, who had his own solo project in production, suggested that The Doobie Brothers reconvene for a final tour, to say 'thank you' to their fans. This started in July 1982 and ran for several weeks, ending at the Greek Theatre in Berkeley, California, on 10-11 September 1982. Tom Johnston, Tiran Porter and John Hartman joined the band for those final two shows. This live album is drawn mostly from those final two nights, as well as from a show a few days beforehand in Universal City. It comprises robust versions of 14 of the band's best-known songs, together with 'Can't Let It Get Away' and 'Olana', two songs that the band had recorded in the studio but had not released on albums. 'Listen To The Music' on this album is sung by Michael McDonald. Live versions of 'You Belong To Me' b/w 'South City Midnight Lady' would be released as a single. The full set-list included solo songs by Simmons (the so-far-unreleased 'Out On The Streets') and McDonald ('I Keep Forgetting', released in August 1982 and heading up the charts as the tour ended).

'If it had to end, that tour and the live album that came of it sure seemed like a good way to go out', Michael McDonald conceded. 'We had always looked forward to every touring season for the longest time, as if we thought it would never end. Notwithstanding our personal struggles and somewhat different histories, this had been our life for most of our early adult years. And now, it was time for whatever was to come next.'

Pat Simmons: 'Watching that crowd go crazy at the end, I thought to myself, 'This is it. This is really the end of the Doobie Brothers.' It was so bittersweet. Part of it was that I don't think we've ever played better. The band were so tight. But things were the way they were. It was one of the greatest moments of my life. But also one of the saddest.'

Another memento of this tour, recorded at the Greek Theater in Berkeley, California, was released as an album and DVD in 2011. These include versions of 'Sweet Maxine', 'Rockin' Down The Highway', 'Take Me In Your Arms (Rock Me A Little While)', 'I Keep Forgettin'', 'Out On The Streets', 'Little Darlin' (I Need You)', 'One Step Closer', 'Dependin' On You' and 'Real Love' not included on the 1983 release. The DVD also includes 'No Stoppin' Us Now'.

On this album, 'Listen To The Music' and 'Long Train Runnin'' are sung by Cornelius Bumpus and 'China Grove' by Tom Johnston.

For now, at least, the three front men of The Doobie Brothers were pursuing solo careers. Tom Johnston toured with his own band, which included fellow Doobie John Hartman on drums. He subsequently formed Border Patrol, which toured the club circuit but did not release any recordings. Michael Hossack and Pat Simmons also worked with the group. Simmons' solo album, *Arcade* (1983), included vocals by Tom Johnston, the top 40 hit single 'So Wrong' and a co-write with Michael McDonald ('Why You Givin' Up'). McDonald also played and sang on a handful of songs. McDonald himself enjoyed success with major singles such as 'I Keep Forgettin' (Every Time You're Near)' (1982, US: 4), 'Yah Mo B There' (with James Ingram, 1985, US: 19), 'Sweet Freedom' (1986, US: 7) and 'On My Own (with Patti LaBelle, US: 1; UK: 2) and the albums *If That's What It Takes* (1982, US: 6) and *No Lookin' Back* (1985, US: 45).

Cycles (1989)

Personnel:
Tom Johnston: vocals, guitar
Patrick Simmons: vocals, guitar
Tiran Porter: bass, backing vocals
John Hartman: drums, backing vocals
Michael Hossack: drums, percussion
Bobby LaKind: percussion, backing vocals
With:
Bill Payne: keyboards
Dave Tyson: keyboards
Kim Bullard: keyboards
Dale Ockerman: keyboards
Phil Aaberg: keyboards
Don Frank: electronic drums
Wayne Jackson: saxophone
Andrew Love: trumpet
Rem Smiers: keytar
Shannon Eigsti: keyboards
Recorded at The Plant, Sausalito, CA, in 1988
Produced by Eddie Schwartz, Charlie Midnight and Rodney Mills
Released: 17 May 1989
Highest chart positions: US: 17, UK: did not chart

With Michael McDonald enjoying a successful solo career, it was perhaps inevitable that The Doobie Brothers would reunite without him. The idea originated with Doobies drummer Keith Knudsen. Knudsen organised a benefit for the National Veterans Foundation on 23 May 1987 at the Hollywood Bowl, with a warm-up show two days before at the San Diego Sports Arena. An impressive lineup of Tom Johnston, Pat Simmons, Jeff Baxter, John McFee, John Hartman, Michael Hossack, Chet McCracken, Michael McDonald, Cornelius Bumpus, Bobby LaKind, Tiran Porter and Ted Templeman joined Keith Knudsen for the show – that's four drummers, two percussionists and four guitar players.

Johnston: 'You could feel the electricity backstage and sense the warmth and camaraderie of a bunch of guys who had been stuck in the trenches together for years. Being in a band really is like that. No matter what, even on those nights when you are at each other's throats, you are going through it together. You will always have those war stories to share with each other. Backstage in San Diego that night, I got the real sense of just how amazing it was that we could all be together to play some music.' The benefit preceded an 11-date tour in May-June 1987. The success of these dates prompted a permanent reunion of the 1972-1974 lineup, which recorded *Toulouse Street, The Captain And Me* and *What Were Once Vices Are Now Habits*, as well as the hit singles 'Listen To The Music', 'Long Train Runnin'', 'China Grove' and 'Black Water'.

'We had done some shows, some benefits,' Tom Johnston told *Guitar Player* in 2024, 'and then some other concerts to pay for those because we were a pretty large band back then. Ted said, 'Why don't you put the original band back together and do another album?' and everybody said, 'Well, sure.' Mike [McDonald] was doing his solo thing, and a couple of the other guys [guitarist John McFee and drummer Keith Knudsen] had Southern Pacific going on, but we had me, Pat, John Hartman, Michael Hossack and Tiran Porter and that was pretty much the original band.'

By 1989, then, The Doobie Brothers were a reunion of survivors from two different eras. *Cycles* manages to sound both like a return to form and – with its glossy, polished instrumentation, processed percussion and clean, linear mix – a calculated embrace of the late-1980s production template. Traces of their middle incarnation remained, including percussionist Bobby LaKind and co-composition credits for former members John McFee, Keith Knudsen and Michael McDonald. It was produced in two sets of sessions. The first, with Eddie Schwartz and Charlie Midnight, provided the hit single 'The Doctor'. The album was completed with Rodney Mills.

Cycles isn't a classic Doobies album in the 1970s sense. It lacks the barnstorming energy of *The Captain And Me* or the cool, studied elegance of *Minute By Minute*. But it does possess a certain charm – a solid, radio-friendly record by a group of musicians who know exactly how to sound like The Doobie Brothers, even if they're not entirely sure what that means in 1989. Where earlier albums felt like the product of shared musical discovery, *Cycles* often sounds like a coordinated effort to remind people what The Doobie Brothers used to sound like. In that sense, it works – but only just.

'The Doctor' (Johnston, Midnight, Schwartz)

Released as a single (with B-side 'Too High A Price') on 3 May 1989. Charts: US: 9. UK: 73.

'I wrote 'The Doctor' when I was playing with a band called Border Patrol', Tom Johnston recalled. 'By the time I took it into the studio for what ended up being *Cycles*, our producers, Charlie Midnight and Eddie Schwartz, had gotten involved with the writing. The initial chord structure was the same as what I'd come up with, but we changed the chorus to what I felt was poppy-sounding. It was not at all what I'd originally come up with, but if we'd done it my way, it wouldn't have sold as it did, so I give them credit for that. They also helped me with the lyrics. I wrote the verses, and we wrote the choruses together.'

As an album opener, 'The Doctor' is a declaration of intent. The guitars are bright and insistent, the tempo upbeat and the chorus irresistibly direct. For Johnston, who had been absent from the group during its McDonald-fronted phase, it marked both a personal and professional return, and he sings with the conviction of someone keen to reclaim centre stage. The lyric may be feather-light, bordering on throwaway, but its unpretentiousness was part of its charm. In the slick, synthesiser-heavy landscape of 1989, a straight-ahead rocker from the Doobies felt almost old-fashioned and perhaps that was its strength: it sounded refreshingly out of step.

Commercially, it worked. The single was a genuine hit in the United States, peaking inside the top ten. For many listeners, it became shorthand for the Doobies' second life. It has endured as the most recognisable track from *Cycles*, outlasting more laboured efforts on the album. Critics noted its simplicity, but Johnston's vocal energy and the band's obvious enthusiasm gave it a sincerity that gloss alone could never supply.

'It's a fun song,' Johnston agreed, 'and I enjoyed doing it in the studio. We recorded it at the Plant in Sausalito, where Fleetwood Mac recorded *Rumours*. A lot of other people did very successful albums there. It was just a fun place to work, and it suited us. Everybody felt good about the album. Next thing, we're back on the road again, and we've never stopped.'

The success of 'The Doctor' set the tone for the reunion. It gave the band's new record label, Capitol, a radio-friendly single to promote and reassured older fans that Johnston's style was not merely intact but thriving. It also allowed the band to tour with something fresh in the set list. Yet, the joy of its creation was tinged with sadness. As Cornelius Bumpus returned to the lineup for the promotional campaign, Bobby LaKind, suffering from terminal cancer, was forced to step aside. His illness would end his life three years later, but in the meantime, the Doobies rallied, staging benefits for his children. In that context, the exuberance of 'The Doctor' carried a bittersweet undertone.

'One Chain (Don't Make No Prison)' (Lambert, Potter)

Released as a single in Canada, Australia and some European territories

The Doobie Brothers' decision to cover 'One Chain' was, on paper, intriguing. Both The Four Tops' original and Santana's muscular version a decade later already gave the song pedigree. The Doobies approached it as both homage and experiment, acknowledging their fondness for soul material while attempting to stamp their own identity onto it. Pat Simmons takes the lead vocal, and he handles it with assurance, his phrasing sympathetic to the Motown source without lapsing into imitation.

The rhythm section lock into a firm groove, with percussion adding texture, and for the first verse and chorus, it feels promising. Yet, as the track unfolds, there is an audible hesitation, as though the band were unsure how far to depart from the template. They play it competently but never entirely commit, resulting in a performance that sits uncomfortably between reverence and reinvention. The potential for a more forceful Doobie Brothers reshaping – layering guitars, pushing the harmonies, driving the beat – remains largely unexplored.

The real obstacle, however, lies in the production. Charlie Midnight and Eddie Schwartz leaned heavily on the studio fashions of 1989, and here the gated drums and synthetic sheen undermine the song's natural rhythmic power. What might have been an earthy, propulsive cover, 'One Chain (Don't Make No Prison)' is trapped inside late-1980s sonics that have not aged well. As a result, 'One Chain' comes across as a curiosity rather than a highlight. It demonstrates the band's stylistic breadth and their continuing respect for black American music, but compared to their more convincing excursions into R&B earlier in their career, this version feels constrained. Its release as a single in selected territories suggests that Capitol were unsure of its wider appeal, and time has confirmed their caution.

'Take Me To The Highway' (Simmons, Ockerman, Fedele, Midnight, Schwartz)

Travel and open roads had long been a Doobie Brothers motif, and 'Take Me To The Highway' tries consciously to revive that tradition. Its bluesy framework, with warm guitar figures and Simmons' steady vocal delivery, gestures towards the freewheeling spirit of earlier road songs. Yet the arrangement keeps glancing nervously towards contemporary polish: there are synth pads where once there would have been Hammond organ, and the backing vocals, pristine and carefully layered, sound very much of 1989.

This tension defines the track. On one hand, it yearns to belong to the lineage of 'Rockin' Down The Highway' or 'Road Angel'; on the other, it is dressed in studio gloss that denies it the rough edges that made those songs breathe. Still, Simmons' vocal carries an easy warmth, and his unforced sincerity helps the track rise above its production. The lyric, though conventional, is delivered with conviction, and there is a pleasing sense of comfort in hearing the Doobies once again evoke the open road.

'Take Me To The Highway' never approaches classic status, but within *Cycles,* it has a quiet appeal. It shows Simmons' knack for shaping material that feels personal, even when surrounded by co-writers, and it provides a reminder of how central his voice had become to the Doobie sound. It is not adventurous, but it does not need to be: its modest strengths lie in familiarity.

'South Of The Border' (Johnston)

Tom Johnston contributes 'South Of The Border', a song that highlights one of the difficulties of *Cycles*: not everything written for the reunion was of equal merit. On paper, a south-of-the-border theme offers possibilities for rhythm, colour and atmosphere, but here the execution is flat. The Latin-inspired groove never fully commits. The percussion is restrained and predictable, leaving the rhythm more suggested than realised. The arrangement is pedestrian, relying on familiar guitar chords and a steady beat that never truly lifts. This is not a bad performance – the players are too professional for that – but it is uninspired. The lyric feels awkward and at times almost embarrassing, with little of the charm or invention Johnston brought to earlier, leaner compositions. When placed alongside the vigour of 'The Doctor' or the soulful promise of 'One Chain', the track feels like filler, assembled quickly to complete the running order. Its lack of ambition is particularly noticeable given the album's broader task of re-establishing the Doobie Brothers as a creative force. In that context, 'South Of The Border' comes across as mechanical, a song that ticks boxes but offers no spark.

'Time Is Here And Gone' (LaKind, McFee, Knudsen)
If any track on *Cycles* hints at the sophistication of the band's McDonald era, it is this one. Co-written by Bobby LaKind, John McFee and Keith Knudsen, 'Time Is Here And Gone' is harmonically richer than most of the album. There are deft chord changes with major sevenths, minor sevenths and added ninths, moments of subtle modulation and a vocal arrangement that suggests the band were aiming for something more contemplative and layered.

Yet, the comparison with the McDonald years is ultimately unflattering. What this track demonstrates most clearly is the absence of his melodic instinct – the knack for finding a line that lingers in the ear long after the song has ended. 'Time Is Here And Gone' aspires to that level of craft but never quite reaches it. The result is polished, carefully constructed and perfectly listenable, but lacking the emotional core that might have elevated it.

In the wider shape of the album, however, the song serves a useful function. It offers contrast, breaking up the sequence of mid-tempo rockers and straightforward covers and suggests that some members of the band were at least interested in exploring subtler textures. As a whole, though, it remains more an exercise in arrangement than a piece of music that truly connects.

'Need A Little Taste Of Love' (Isley, Isley, Isley, Isley, Isley, Jasper)
Released as a single (with B-side 'I Can Read Your Mind') in 1989. Charts: US: 45. An extended remix appeared on the CD single of 'One Chain'
Covering the Isley Brothers was a bold move. Their catalogue is both revered and definitive, and stepping into that territory risks exposing limitations. On 'Need A Little Taste Of Love', the Doobies give it a respectable try. Tom Johnston takes the vocal, delivering with enthusiasm if not with the effortless soul of the original. The band fall into a pleasing groove, echoing the shuffle of 'Eyes Of Silver' from the mid-70s, and for a moment, it feels like familiar ground.

The trouble is that the track, while pleasant, lacks authority. It sounds less like a confident reinterpretation and more like a bar-band approximation – competent, enjoyable, but not necessary. Within the context of a comeback album, it raises questions about intent: was this really the material on which the Doobies wanted to re-establish themselves? The inclusion of a cover is not a problem in itself – *Toulouse Street* had proved how effective that could be – but here the choice feels more like padding than statement.

'I Can Read Your Mind' (Simmons, Ockerman, Thompson)
Co-written with the band's touring keyboardist Dale Ockerman, 'I Can Read Your Mind' has the air of a carefully crafted mid-tempo pop-rock single, aimed squarely at late-1980s radio. It opens with an inviting guitar figure, develops into a smooth chorus and adds just enough production gloss to sound contemporary without being overwhelming. The attempt to echo the blue-eyed soul of the McDonald era is unmistakable. The rhythm is restrained, the backing vocals silky, the atmosphere polite. Yet what is missing is the spark of individuality that McDonald's voice and melodic sense once supplied. Instead, the track settles for competence: neat guitar interplay, a solid hook and a tone that is radio-ready but emotionally shallow. For Simmons, it was another opportunity to step forward as a writer, and his vocal performance is warm and sympathetic. Listened to in isolation, the track is by no means poor, but in the context of the Doobies' catalogue, it is minor, one of those professional but forgettable songs that pass by without much trace.

'Tonight I'm Coming Through (The Border)' (LaKind, McDonald)
The presence of Michael McDonald as a co-writer inevitably raises expectations. Could this be the point where the reunion album connects more directly with the band's hugely successful late-1970s sound? In practice, the answer is no. 'Tonight I'm Coming Through (The Border)' is a heavy-handed rocker, propelled by a rhythm section drenched in late-1980s reverb. Johnston and Simmons share the vocal duties, and both acquit themselves professionally, but the song itself is pedestrian. The chorus, while structured correctly, feels forced, as if meeting contractual requirements for a rock anthem. The title promises drama and intrigue, yet the music trudges along dutifully, never truly catching fire.

What is most striking is how un-McDonald-like it sounds. His co-writing credit suggests input at an earlier stage, but any trace of his melodic or harmonic fingerprint is faint. Instead, the track feels like an obligation – an attempt to harness star power without much substance behind it.

'Wrong Number' (Johnston)
'Wrong Number' offers Tom Johnston another chance to front a rocker, and this time, he aims for something both playful and faintly sinister. The shuffle rhythm is familiar, recalling earlier Doobie patterns, and the harmonica adds a touch of colour. There is an attempt at humour in the lyric, but it never quite lands, and the menace hinted at in the arrangement feels half-hearted. As with 'South Of The Border', the impression is of a song assembled competently but without inspiration. Johnston's return to the band had re-energised him on 'The Doctor', but not every idea carried that same vitality. 'Wrong Number' illustrates the danger of leaning too heavily on formula: what once sounded effortless now sounds laboured.

'Too High A Price' (LaKind, Zirngiebel, Herron)
The album closes with 'Too High A Price', co-written by Bobby LaKind with Zeke Zirngiebel (from Warren Zevon's band) and John Herron. Designed as a reflective ending, it begins with understated harmonies and verses that suggest genuine thoughtfulness. For a moment, it appears the Doobies may finish on a mature, subtle note. But the chorus takes a different turn, lunging into AOR bombast better suited to the likes of Journey or Foreigner. The contrast is jarring, as if two separate songs have been awkwardly joined. Pat Simmons pushes his voice to the upper edge of his range, which adds strain rather than drama. His brief guitar solo is a welcome highlight – taut, expressive and more convincing than the material around it – but it is not enough to rescue the track.

In many ways, 'Too High A Price' encapsulates the weaknesses of *Cycles*. For all the professionalism on display, the band occasionally lost sight of what made their best work distinctive. Here, the connective tissue between past and present is absent. The Doobie Brothers always managed, even at their most experimental, to sound unmistakably themselves. On this closer, that identity slips away, leaving a song that could have been performed by almost any AOR act of the period. Even dedicated fans are unlikely to return to it often.

Related Track
Cycles was reissued in 2002 by One Way Records with two bonus tracks, namely the extended mix of 'Need A Little Taste Of Love' and 'Anything For Love'.

'Anything For Love' (LaKind, Schwartz, Zirngiebel)
This track originally appeared on the CD single of 'The Doctor'. It's a glossy, mid-tempo power ballad that feels custom-built for late-night FM radio rotation and soft-rock countdowns.

Brotherhood (1991)

Personnel:
Tom Johnston: vocals, guitars
Patrick Simmons: vocals, guitars
Tiran Porter: bass, vocals
John Hartman: drums
Michael Hossack: drums, percussion
With
Steve Canali: slide guitar
Jimi Fox: percussion
Dale Ockerman: keyboards
Richard Bryant, Vicki Randle and Rem Smiers: background vocals
Recorded at The Plant, Sausalito and Image Recording, Hollywood, in 1990
Produced by Rodney Mills
Released 15 April 1991
Highest chart positions. US: 82. UK: did not chart

1989's *Cycles* was a carefully managed reunion project aimed at recapturing past glories. It saw some success, with a top 20 chart placing and a major hit single. The band's second album for Capitol, *Brotherhood*, feels like a band increasingly unsure of its place in a shifting musical landscape. Grunge was at the gates, and adult-oriented rock – especially that made by bands now two decades past their prime – was losing traction. Ten years hence, the legacy circuit would be *in situ,* and The Doobie Brothers would find their place there (and record two of their best albums as a happy consequence).

Brotherhood is a competent if ultimately conservative attempt to stay commercially relevant, pairing slick production (Rodney Mills back in the chair) with familiar lyrical tropes: the road, love, regret, redemption. It's a glossy, well-played record, but one that too often sacrifices inspiration for professionalism. The musicianship is impeccable, the arrangements polished, the production professional – but the spark of danger or discovery is largely absent. It's an album made by excellent players and lots of songwriters trying to meet expectations rather than defy them. For completists, it's a comforting listen. For others, it's proof that technical ability cannot always substitute for inspiration. The result is an album that neither offends nor excites.

The track listing features outside writers on seven of the ten songs; four tracks included no composing contributions by the group at all. It was their first album to miss the top 20 since their debut, 20 years before. As a consequence, long-time bassist Tiran Porter left for a solo career, never to return (he released a fascinating but flawed funk-tinged progressive rock outing called *Playing To An Empty House* in 1995). Original drummer John Hartman quit music altogether, and Capitol dropped the band. It would be another nine years before the next studio album by The Doobie Brothers.

'Something You Said' (Lunn, Gorrie)
If the drums were buried in reverb on *Cycles,* then hold my beer. 'Something You Said' is an up-tempo opener that sets the tone – melodic, lively and just a bit too safe. It was co-written by Alan Gorrie of Average White Band and Michael Lunn, who penned tunes for Starship and Lynyrd Skynyrd (another band who were trying to revive their career in the early 1990s). The chorus is pleasant without being memorable, but the arrangement feels a little too polished. It's a promising beginning that never quite lifts off.

'Is Love Enough' (Williams, Richmond)
Tom Johnston takes the mic for a more energetic number, which steers too close to the riff that drives Stevie Wonder's 'Superstition'. The question he asks – 'Is love enough?' – is never convincingly answered. The guitar work is tight, the chorus harmonies rich, but the song feels like a template exercise in AOR songwriting. Here we point to Jerry Lynn Williams, author of several songs for Eric Clapton's massive album *Journeyman* (1989), and Walk Richmond, who had worked with Michael Bolton and would place a song on 1991's Bob Seger album. Like much of the album, 'Is Love Enough' is expertly built but emotionally vacant.

'Dangerous' (Simmons)
Released as a single (edited) (with B-side 'Our Love') in 1991. Charts: did not chart.
'Dangerous' successfully reintroduces some grit and menace to the Doobies' sound. Starting with some scintillating dobro playing, it bursts into an electric guitar riff, which is strong, the vocal straining for urgency. But there's a laboured feel here, as if the band are overcompensating for the album's smoothness elsewhere. Not bad, but self-conscious.

'Our Love' (Williams)
This syrupy ballad was written by Jerry Lynn Williams. Tom Johnson's delivery is tender, and the harmonies are typically immaculate. But structurally, it treads water. There's a sense that it belongs more to a 1980s Chicago or REO Speedwagon record than one by The Doobie Brothers.

'Divided Highway' (Simmons, Fox, Peterik)
Perhaps the album's most energetic (and typical) track on *Brotherhood*, 'Divided Highway' has a chugging rhythm that recalls the band's early 1970s rockers. Unfortunately, it also suffers from generic road-song syndrome, trading originality for clichés about wheels, signs and destinations. Still, it's one of the few tracks that sounds like the band are enjoying themselves.

It's the first of two writing contributions by Jim Peterik of the band Survivor, who had broken up a couple of years before, having gifted 'Eye Of The Tiger' to the world.

'Under The Spell' (Peterik, Syniar, Wertico)
A curious mid-album shift that is darker, more atmospheric and vaguely bluesy. Pat Simmons is in fine voice, but the melody never quite coalesces. The co-writers are a curious mix of 1980s AOR (Jim Peterik and Bill Syniar of Survivor) and cool jazz (Paul Wertico worked with Pat Metheny Group for 18 years).

'Excited' (Johnston, Williams)
Despite its title, this is a somewhat listless slice of synth-tinged rock. The tempo is upbeat, the chorus passable, but the arrangement sounds oddly dated, even for 1991. One could easily mistake it for a leftover from *Cycles* and not a particularly strong one. It sounded much better as part of the band's live concerts.

'This Train I'm On' (Simmons, Ockerman)
A modest highlight, with Pat Simmons returning to more familiar ground with slide guitar, rhythmic invention and warm harmonies. The lyrics are tinged with quiet resignation. While it doesn't break new ground, it at least sounds authentically Doobie-esque.

'Showdown' (Johnston)
'Showdown' is a funk-inflected guitar workout with big drums and bravado to match. Tom Johnston does his best to summon urgency, but the lyric borders on parody ('It's a showdown, better get ready, it's showdown!'). It feels like something recorded with one eye on the live set list rather than the album sequence.

'Rollin' On' (Johnston)
The closer attempts to end things on an optimistic, vaguely rootsy note. The acoustic guitars and Hammond organ return, the harmonies settle into an easy groove and the sentiment is warm, if well-worn. It's the best song on the album by some distance, merely because the band are not trying to be something they're not. It's an uplifting farewell, both to the album and, unintentionally, to this era of the band itself.

Listen To The Music: The Very Best Of The Doobie Brothers (1993)

Released 24 May 1993
Highest chart positions. US: did not chart. UK: did not chart
Track listing: 'Long Train Runnin'', 'China Grove', 'Listen To The Music', 'Takin' It To The Streets', 'Black Water', 'Jesus Is Just Alright', 'Rockin' Down The Highway', 'Take Me In Your Arms (Rock Me A Little While)', 'Without You', 'South City Midnight Lady', 'It Keeps You Runnin'', 'Little Darling (I Need You)', 'You Belong To Me', 'Minute By Minute', 'Here To Love You', 'Real Love', 'What A Fool Believes', 'Long Train Runnin' (Locomotive Remix '93)', 'Listen To The Music (Motiv8 7' Edit)'

By 1993, the compact disc boom was in full swing and with it came a tidal wave of greatest hits compilations. Every major label was rifling through its archives, repackaging familiar names with slightly altered artwork and generous hyperbole. In this climate, *Listen To The Music: The Very Best Of The Doobie Brothers* should have been a commercial slam dunk. It wasn't. Despite being a big hit in Australia and New Zealand, the collection sank without a trace in both the US and UK charts – an outcome that seems baffling on the surface, given the ubiquity of the band's classic hits and the then-booming nostalgia market.

A closer look reveals an all-too-familiar story: a compilation assembled by committee, marketed without enthusiasm and curated with a curious blend of caution and indecision. The track list is, on paper, unimpeachable: 'China Grove', 'Long Train Runnin'', 'Listen To The Music', 'What A Fool Believes', 'Minute By Minute', 'Takin' It To The Streets' – all present and accounted for. And yet, the sequence lacks drama or shape. Tracks are ordered neither chronologically nor in thematic fashion, making for a listening experience that is oddly flat despite the quality of the material. What's more, the compilation offers no new material other than two horrendous remixes (both of which would enter the UK singles charts; 'Long Train Runnin'' reached number seven in November 1993 and 'Listen To The Music' would peak at number 37 during a four-week run in May-June 1994). The sleeve notes are perfunctory, the design generic. This CD feels like a petrol station impulse buy – serviceable but entirely lacking in prestige.

So why did *Listen To The Music* fail to chart in the US or UK? Timing and presentation both play a role. In 1993, there was no anniversary to mark, no reunion to publicise and no television campaign to drive sales. This was not a lovingly curated retrospective – it was a contractual compilation, dropped into a saturated market with the enthusiasm of a shrug. The Doobie Brothers deserved better. So did their audience.

Rockin' Down The Highway: The Wildlife Concert (1996)

Personnel:
Tom Johnston: vocals, guitars
Patrick Simmons: vocals, guitars
John McFee: backing vocals, guitars, slide guitar, pedal steel guitar, violin
Michael Hossack: drums
Keith Knudsen: backing vocals, drums
With:
Michael McDonald: vocals and keyboards
Cornelius Bumpus: vocals, saxophones, flute, keyboards
Skylark: backing vocals, bass
Danny Hull: backing vocals, saxophones, harmonica, keyboards, percussion
Dale Ockerman: backing vocals, keyboards
Carlos Guaico and Buck Johnson: backing vocals, percussion
Recorded on 5 and 6 May 1996 at Sony Music Studios, New York and 11 May 1996 at Starwood Amphitheater, Nashville, TN
Produced by The Doobie Brothers and Charlie Midnight
Released: July 1996
Highest chart positions: US: did not chart, UK: did not chart.
Track listing: 'Dangerous', 'Jesus Is Just Alright', 'Take Me In Your Arms (Rock Me A Little While)', 'Slow Burn', 'Dependin' On You', 'Another Park, Another Sunday', 'The Doctor', 'Slack Key Soquel Rag', 'South City Midnight Lady', 'Eyes Of Silver', 'Black Water', 'Takin' It To The Streets', 'Rockin' Down The Highway', 'Minute By Minute', 'Wild Ride', 'China Grove', 'Dark Eyed Cajun Woman', 'Neal's Fandango', 'Without You', 'Clear As The Driven Snow', 'Excited', 'What A Fool Believes', 'Long Train Runnin'', 'Listen To The Music'

The Doobie Brothers toured each year after their *Brotherhood* album. In 1993, Keith Knudsen and John McFee rejoined on a full-time basis after their band Southern Pacific disbanded after eight years and four albums. They reunited with Bumpus and McDonald in 1995 for a co-headlining tour with the Steve Miller Band. In 1996, they performed two benefit concerts for the Wildlife Conservation Society. The album that documents these shows is strong, with a well-drilled live lineup that now included the terrific new bassist Skylark. The entire concert is available on the band's YouTube channel. It's worth watching just for Pat Simmons' bangs.

Some parts of the album were recorded at Starwood Amphitheater, Nashville, TN, on 11 May 1996, when the band supported Lynyrd Skynyrd. Michael McDonald guests on excellent versions of 'Takin' It To The Streets', 'Minute By Minute' and 'What A Fool Believes'. It was re-released a few years later as *Best Of The Doobie Brothers Live,* with several songs omitted. The album doesn't really add anything to the band's wider oeuvre, but it shows a super-tight live band starting to emerge from 'trying to be relevant' into 'appreciating their legacy'.

Two tracks had not previously appeared on the group's albums.

'Slow Burn' (Johnston, McFee, Knudsen, Hossack)
'Slow Burn' was a new track co-written by four of the band members. Over a slinky bass line, ringing guitars and grizzled harmonica, 'Slow Burn' fits right into the set list. Yes, we might have heard variants of the arrangement and sentiment on several other songs over the previous albums, but one cannot deny the commitment.

'Wild Ride' (Simmons, Midnight)
'Wild Ride' had been the opening track on Pat Simmons' second solo album, *Take Me To The Highway,* released in Japan the same year. This revisits some classic Doobie Brothers music ('Black Water', 'Long Train Runnin'', 'Listen To The Music') and a few of Pat's solo recordings. It's now very rare (or very expensive, depending on your perspective). 'Wild Ride' is a fine song, a bluesy shuffle with some of Simmons' intriguing dynamics.

Long Train Runnin': 1970-2000 (1999)

Released: September 1999
Highest chart positions: US: did not chart, UK: did not chart
Track list: 'Nobody (Single Version)', 'Slippery St. Paul', 'Listen To The Music (Single Version)', 'Rockin' Down The Highway (Single Version)', 'Toulouse Street', 'Cotton Mouth', 'Jesus Is Just Alright', 'White Sun', 'Natural Thing', 'Long Train Runnin'', 'China Grove', 'Dark Eyed Cajun Woman', 'Clear As The Driven Snow', 'South City Midnight Lady', 'You Just Can't Stop It', 'Spirit', 'Pursuit On 53rd St.', 'Black Water', 'Eyes Of Silver', 'Down In The Track', 'Another Park, Another Sunday', 'Sweet Maxine (Single Version)', 'Neal's Fandango', 'Music Man', 'Slack Key Soquel Rag', 'Take Me In Your Arms (Rock Me A Little While)', 'Texas Lullaby', 'I Cheat The Hangman', 'Wheels Of Fortune (Single Version)', 'Losin' End', 'Takin' It To The Streets', 'It Keeps You Runnin'', 'Echoes Of Love', 'Nothin' But A Heartache', 'Chinatown', 'There's A Light', 'Little Darling (I Need You)', 'You Belong To Me', 'Open Your Eyes', 'Minute By Minute', 'Dependin' On You', 'Don't Stop To Watch The Wheels', 'What A Fool Believes', 'Here To Love You (Single Version)', 'Dedicate This Heart', 'Real Love', 'No Stoppin' Us Now', 'One Step Closer', 'Keep This Train A-Rollin'', 'South Bay Strut', 'One By One', 'Wynken, Blynken And Nod', 'The Doctor', 'South Of The Border', 'Time Is Here And Gone', 'Need A Little Taste Of Love', 'Dangerous', 'Excited', 'This Train I'm On', 'Rollin' On', 'Little Bitty Pretty One', 'Daughters Of The Sea (Demo)', 'Armadillo Death Chant', 'Osborne (Long Train Runnin')', 'Four Days Gone', 'Spiel', 'Lovin' My Way Back Home', 'Pat's Song', 'Bluejay', 'Peace In The Valley', 'Mambo Waltz', 'Outside Of Barstow', 'Argentine Grape (Sweet Maxine)', 'Shuffle (Double Dealin' Four Flusher)', 'Takin' It To The Streets (Demo)', 'We Would Sail Away (St. Paul)', 'Jesus Is Just Alright (Live Version, 1982)', 'Olana'

It was perhaps inevitable that The Doobie Brothers would compile and issue a multi-disc box set. *Long Train Runnin': 1970-2000* was released on 14 September 1999 and comprises between four and seven tracks from each of their albums released between 1972 and 1991 (seven from nine songs on *One Step Closer* is a generous allocation), along with two tracks from their debut. Collectors could also enjoy the single mixes of 'Nobody', 'Listen To The Music', 'Rockin' Down The Highway', 'Sweet Maxine', 'Wheels Of Fortune' and 'Here To Love You'. And while this collection doesn't always justify its own scale, it makes a valiant effort to reframe The Doobie Brothers not just as a singles band, but as a band of phases, moods and continuity, however elusive. Yes, all the hits are here. But things become slightly more curious around the margins. Tracks like 'Wynken, Blynken And Nod' and 'Need A Little Taste Of Love' (from 1989's *Cycles*) suggest a desire to dig a little deeper into the catalogue. Plus, there is one new track and several unreleased songs from 1971, 1974 and 1982.

'Little Bitty Pretty One' (Day)
The sleeve notes say that 'Little Bitty Pretty One' would be released on 'the forthcoming album on Pyramid Records', namely 2000's *Sibling Rivalry*. It

was, but only as a bonus track for the Japanese market. 'Little Bitty Pretty One' is a 1957 song written and originally recorded by Bobby Day. That same year, the song was popularised by Thurston Harris. It's a straightforward, old-fashioned rock 'n' roll song with doo wop harmonies, which formed part of the band's set list for years.

'Daughters Of The Sea' (Simmons)
'Armadillo Death Chant' (Johnston)
'Osborne' (Johnston)
'Four Days Gone' (Simmons)
Recorded at Wally Heider Recording Studio, Los Angeles, CA, on 9 July 1971
These are early sessions for the band's second album. At this stage, they a still a four-piece with bassist Dave Shogren. These are competent and interesting, but hardly set the world on fire. 'Daughters Of The Sea' is a demo of a song that was subsequently re-recorded for *What Were Once Vices Are Now Habits*. 'Osbourne' is an early version of 'Long Train Runnin''.

'Spiel' (Hartman)
'Lovin' My Way Back Home' (Johnston)
'Pat's Song' (Simmons)
'Bluejay' (Johnston)
'Peace In The Valley' (Johnston)
Recorded at Wally Heider Studios, San Francisco, CA, between September and October 1971
These are five further self-produced recordings by the original four-piece lineup. Bassist Dave Shogren would leave The Doobie Brothers immediately after these sessions, disillusioned by a lack of focus. This is exemplified by 'Spiel', which explains why John Hartman did not write many songs for The Doobie Brothers. Other than this throwaway, this is a strong set of recordings. 'Pat's Song' is quite lovely: top-class acoustic guitar picking. 'Bluejay' could easily have been included on *Toulouse Street*.

'Mambo Waltz' (Simmons)
'Outside Of Barstow' (Johnston)
'Argentine Grape' (Simmons, Johnston)
'Shuffle' (Simmons)
Recorded at Warner Bros. Studios, N. Hollywood, CA, between August and November 1974
Here we have four outtakes from the sessions for *Stampede*. 'Mambo Waltz' is another of Pat Simmons' acoustic interludes. One assumes that 'Slack Key Soquel Rag' was given the nod. 'Outside Of Barstow' is an acoustic blues shuffle which simply seems undercooked. 'Argentine Grape' is an early version of 'Sweet Maxine', which badly misses Bill Payne's piano flourishes. 'Shuffle' is a harder, faster take of 'Double Dealin' Four Flusher'.

'Takin' It To The Streets' (McDonald)
'We Would Sail Away (St. Paul)' (McDonald)
These demos, recorded on 21 November 1975, comprise just Michael McDonald's piano and vocals – one can really appreciate his depth of compositional and performance skill. 'Taking It To The Streets' is a pleasantly stripped-back but effortlessly powerful arrangement. 'We Would Sail Away (St. Paul)' is a masterpiece, as McDonald channels Randy Newman mixed with a stunning gospel vocal performance.

'Jesus Is Just Alright' (Reynolds)
This live version was recorded on the band's farewell tour in 1982.

'Olana' (McDonald)
'Olana' was written and sung by Michael McDonald. It's an uneasy mix of loud guitars and 1980s shimmering keyboards. The sleeve notes for 'Olana' note that the song was recorded in January 1983. This seems unlikely, as the band's farewell tour had taken place in July-September 1982. Early or mid-1982 seems a more likely timeframe.

Sibling Rivalry (2000)

Personnel:
Tom Johnston: vocals, guitars
Patrick Simmons: vocals, guitars, banjo
John McFee: vocals, guitars, dobro, pedal steel guitar, harmonica, violin, mandolin
Keith Knudsen: vocals, drums, percussion
Michael Hossack: drums, percussion
With:
Guy Allison: keyboards, background vocals
Mario Cippolina, John Cowan, George Hawkins Jr: bass
Bob Bangerter: acoustic guitar
Marc Russo: horn, saxophone
Chris Thompson, Maxayn Lewis, Yvonne Williams, Bill Champlin, Cris Sommer-Simmons, Lil' Patrick Harley Simmons: background vocals
Recorded at Lizard Rock, Solvang, California; Earth Walk, Agoura Hills, California; Capitol, Hollywood, California; Hyberbolic and Tom Hall's Melody Line Studios, Maui, Hawaii, between 1999 and 2000
Produced by Guy Allison, Terry Nelson and The Doobie Brothers
Released: 3 October 2000
Highest chart positions: US: did not chart, UK: did not chart

Nine years is a long time between albums. By the time *Sibling Rivalry* was released in October 2000, the musical landscape had shifted tectonically. Grunge had come and gone, hip-hop ruled the airwaves and boy bands were selling CDs by the truckload. So, what were The Doobie Brothers doing back in the studio? The answer lies in *Sibling Rivalry*, a curious and often overlooked chapter in their storied discography.

Sibling Rivalry is not a comeback album in the traditional sense. It doesn't attempt to recapture the magic of *Toulouse Street* or *Minute By Minute*, nor does it aggressively modernise. Instead, it offers a tapestry of adult-oriented rock from a band that has nothing left to prove. Yes, it's uneven. Yes, it's a bit long at 13 tracks. But scattered among the genre experiments and polished production are moments of real songwriting craft and musical depth.

'People Gotta Love Again' (Johnston)

The album opens with a statement of intent. Tom Johnson's gruff vocals return like a familiar friend, offering a socially conscious lyric that feels both earnest and just a touch anachronistic. The production reflects the era: clean and polished with a bright, precise sound. The arpeggiated keyboards in the chorus are entirely superfluous. Thankfully, these don't overwhelm, but they do sound out of place. More welcome is John McFee's violin solo, which adds a hint of a rustic timbre. There's a pseudo-reggae lilt to the rhythm, a style the Doobies flirted with in the past, but here it's slightly more subdued. 'People

Gotta Love Again' shows their desire to stay relevant while remaining true to themselves. It's a winner. The songwriting is mature, almost Springsteenian in its blue-collar introspection. The production is tastefully restrained, allowing the song's emotion to breathe. One of the album's hidden gems, deserving of more attention than it received.

'Leave My Heartache Behind' (Simmons)
Pat Simmons leads this mid-tempo acoustic rocker with a lyric about liberation and renewal. It's musically reminiscent of 'Black Water', which is not a bad thing, and the playing and production are sublime. It's songs like this that remind us why Pat Simmons was and is such an important part of The Doobie Brothers.

'Ordinary Man' (Bangerter, Ruff, Bequette)
Released as a single in 2001. Charts: did not chart.
This is something of a self-indulgence. Pat Simmons steps into the spotlight with a slow, soulful ballad that screams 'Michael McDonald' or *Pilgrim*-era Eric Clapton. It's all Fender Rhodes, tasteful jazz guitar and Hammond organ. The co-composers are Simmons' fellow Hawaii residents, jazz guitarist Bob Bangerter and keyboard player Michael Ruff. The lyrics are by Bangerter's wife, Neida Bequette. It's very pleasant, but even for a band who pushed the boundaries as much as The Doobies, this seems very out of character.

'Jericho' (Johnston)
There are modern production twists on Tom Johnson's 'Jericho' (they called it 'hip hop' in contemporary interviews, which it isn't). These chime awkwardly with the taut drums, pumping horns and funky guitars. There's a welcome gospel edge to the backing – appropriate for a song about biblical walls falling – and the harmonies are sublime. You must, however, put your expectations in your pocket for this one.

'On Every Corner' (Knudsen, Zirngiebel)
A third writing credit for Zeke Zirngiebel in late-period Doobies. We have a welcome, relaxed lead vocal turn for Keith Knudsen, who always had a fine set of pipes: he would sing 'Listen To The Music' in live concerts in the post-Johnson lineup. The chorus is classic Doobies, with massed vocal harmonies and an uplifting melody. The issue with the song is that, despite the professionalism on display, it's not particularly in character nor very memorable.

'Angels Of Madness' (Allison, Hossack, McFee)
There's a strong argument that the band's ace up their sleeve over the last 30 years is guitarist John McFee, who returned in 1993 in an official capacity after an11-year absence. His 'Angels Of Madness' is arguably the best adult pop song

they've put out since the door closed behind Michael McDonald. This is McFee's only lead vocal for the band. It's also the first of three co-writing credits on this album for Guy Allison, the touring keyboardist for the Doobie Brothers from 1996 to 2015 (19 years with the band and just one album).

'45th Floor' (Champlin, Johnston)
Tom Johnston kicks things back into life with '45th Floor'. The band sound tight and the guitar interplay is classic Doobies – twin rhythms, sly fills and the kind of groove they always made seem effortless. The riff is familiar, the rhythm is steady, and while it doesn't break new ground, it proves the band can still lock into a groove as well as they ever did. The song was co-written by Bill Champlin, a member of the rock band Chicago from 1981 to 2009, who also has his own well-regarded band, Sons Of Champlin.

'Can't Stand To Lose' (Cowan, Young)
Here, the Doobies dip into country-rock, with Pat Simmons purring through a soppy ballad. Its piano, strings and wordless backing vocals remind the listener of 'Wasted Time' by The Eagles. The song is co-written by Rusty Young of Poco (who co-incidentally gifted two musicians to The Eagles) and John Cowan, who toured as bassist and vocalist with The Doobie Brothers between 1993 and 1995 and has been ever-present since 2010.

'Higher Ground' (Champlin, Champlin, Johnston)
Not the Stevie Wonder song. Instead, this is a mid-tempo rocker with a catchy refrain, a big chorus and ambitions it can't quite achieve. Chris Thompson of Manfred Mann's Earth Band contributes to the writing. It's a departure from the Doobies' usual fare – more AOR than classic rock – but competently executed. Perhaps recording the Steve Wonder song might have been a better idea.

'Gates Of Eden' (Allison, Knudsen)
Keith Knudsen co-writes and sings another mid-tempo AOR number, exploring spiritual themes. It's a reflective power ballad that wouldn't feel out of place on a late-period Eagles album. John McFee's violin seems desperately out of place amid the flag-waving, Zippo-waving choruses.

'Don't Be Afraid' (Simmons, Sommer-Simmons, Bangerter)
'Don't Be Afraid' trips into a contemporary Latin jazz booby trap. Like 'Ordinary Man', it was co-written by Bob Bangerter and with a credit for Pat Simmons' wife, Cris. It's a brave inclusion, entirely off the Doobies' beaten path. For some, it will be a welcome breath of fresh air; for others, a curious misstep.

'Rocking Horse' (Allison, Knudsen)
A return to meat-and-potatoes rock, with snarling vocals, a head-nodding groove and touches of funk. This track tries hard to inject some late-album

energy, and while it succeeds in part, it also feels a bit by-the-numbers. Still, there's always something reassuring about Tom Johnston shouting over a chunky riff. With Johnston and McFee tearing into some wailing leads, this song just about manages to lift the album out of the slumbers.

'Five Corners' (McFee, Simmons)
A solid and breezy acoustic instrumental by John McFee and Pat Simmons. These guys are phenomenal musicians, there's no doubt. Yes, this comes off as son-of-'Slippery St. Paul', but who cares when the music is as classy as this?

The Japanese release also includes a bonus track, 'Little Bitty Pretty One', which had been released in 1999 on the *Long Train Runnin'* box set.

Greatest Hits (2001)

Released: 4 September 2001
Highest chart positions: US: 142, UK: 45
Track listing: 'Listen To The Music', 'Jesus Is Just Alright', 'Rockin' Down The Highway', 'Long Train Runnin'', 'Without You', 'China Grove', 'Nobody', 'Black Water', 'Take Me In Your Arms (Rock Me A Little While)', 'It Keeps You Runnin'', 'Takin' It To The Streets', 'You Belong To Me', 'Echoes Of Love', 'What A Fool Believes', 'Minute By Minute', 'Dependin' On You', 'One Step Closer', 'Real Love', 'The Doctor', 'Dangerous'

By 2001, the compact disc market had matured into what might be called its 'historical' phase – labels were no longer simply repackaging music for convenience, but for legacy. And few labels handled that business with more curatorial precision than Rhino Records. Where Warner Bros.' 1993 *Listen To The Music* compilation felt perfunctory, Rhino's *Greatest Hits* arrives as something more substantial: a thoughtful, expansive and long-overdue reckoning with one of America's most durable – and most stylistically bifurcated – bands.

This time, the title is not a marketing euphemism. This is, at last, the very best, and crucially, it's the first compilation that embraces the full extent of The Doobie Brothers' peculiar dual identity: from denim-clad biker bar boogie to sophisticated blue-eyed soul. This collection makes no effort to sanitise or segregate the band's two major eras. Instead, it treats the Tom Johnston-led roots rock and Michael McDonald-era jazz-pop with equal weight and respect. In so doing, Rhino presents the band not as a group that changed course midstream, but as one that evolved with curiosity and conviction, even at the cost of coherence.

If *Listen To The Music: The Very Best Of The Doobie Brothers* was a cash-in compilation, convenient but lifeless, then Rhino's 2001 edition is an act of musical historiography. It presents the Doobie Brothers as more than just a radio band or a Michael McDonald launching pad; it reveals them as a shape shifting collective of real breadth and surprising emotional range. This is not just a better compilation – it's a better argument. For anyone still asking whether The Doobie Brothers deserve a place in the classic rock pantheon, *Greatest Hits* answers with a firm 'yes'.

For the record, a two-disc *The Very Best Of The Doobie Brothers* would follow in March 2007, comprising 33 songs taken from all of their albums to date. In the interim, 2002's *Doobie's Choice* compiled 20 non-hits, and the same year's *Divided Highway* collected 16 of the 20 tracks from the band's two albums for Capitol, which smacks of barrel scraping.

Live At Wolf Trap (2004)

Personnel:
Tom Johnston: guitars, vocals
John McFee: guitars, dobro, pedal steel guitar, harmonica, violin, mandolin, vocals
Patrick Simmons: guitars, banjo, vocals
Michael Hossack: drums, percussion
Keith Knudsen: drums, percussion, vocals
With:
Guy Allison: keyboards, vocals, background vocals
Skylark: bass, background vocals
M. B. Gordy: percussion
Marvin McFadden: trumpet
Mic Gillette: trombone, trumpet
Marc Russo: saxophone
Produced by Michael Drumm and Andrea Allen
Released: 26 October 2004
Highest chart positions: US: did not chart, UK: did not chart
Track listing: 'Rockin' Down The Highway', 'Jesus Is Just Alright', 'Dangerous', 'Another Park, Another Sunday', 'Steamer Lane', 'South City Midnight Lady', 'Snake Man', 'Five Corners', 'Rainy Day Crossroad Blues', 'Clear As The Driven Snow', 'Don't Start Me Talkin'', 'Take Me In Your Arms (Rock Me A Little While)', 'Little Bitty Pretty One', 'Black Water', 'Long Train Runnin'', 'China Grove', 'Listen To The Music'

By 2004, The Doobie Brothers were well into their so-called 'heritage act' years – a phrase that often belies the continued vitality of bands with nothing left to prove but everything still to play for. *Live At Wolf Trap*, recorded in the summer of 2004, is not so much a victory lap as it is a carefully curated retrospective: 22 tracks, two hours, five seasoned players, three lead vocalists and, crucially, not a whiff of apology. This is the Doobies in full flight: road-hardened, rhythmically locked and gleefully unburdened by the need to reinvent the wheel. And yet, *Wolf Trap* is no museum piece – it's a living, breathing document of a band that still believe in the spiritual power of a well-executed groove. Much of this can be attributed to the band's bassist, Skylark, who had played with them for over ten years at this point.

There are no major surprises in the set list, but there are plenty of pleasures. Of course, the elephant in the amphitheatre is Michael McDonald. His absence is neither acknowledged nor felt too keenly, though songs like 'Takin' It To The Streets' and 'Minute By Minute' are conspicuously omitted. Perhaps wisely, the band choose not to dabble in that more soul-inflected era – this is the boogie band, not the balladeers. One wonders what a guest appearance might've added. Then again, perhaps *Live At Wolf Trap* is stronger for knowing exactly what it is and sticking to it.

Drummer Keith Knudsen died suddenly the year after this release. The Doobie Brothers sang 'Jesus Is Just Alright' at his memorial service.

World Gone Crazy (2010)

Personnel:
Tom Johnston: vocals, guitars
Pat Simmons: vocals, guitars
John McFee: backing vocals, guitars, banjo, mandolin, violin, drums, percussion
Michael Hossack: drums, percussion
With:
Michael McDonald: vocals
Willie Nelson: vocals
Ross Hogarth: guitar, drums, percussion
Tim Pierce: guitar
Bob Glaub: bass
James Hutchinson: bass
Gregg Bissonette: drums
Joey Waronker: drums
Karl Perazzo: percussion
Ted Templeman: tambourine
Guy Allison: piano, Wurlitzer electric piano, Hammond organ
Bill Payne: piano, Hammond organ
Kim Bullard: synthesiser, keyboards, piano
Norton Buffalo: harmonica
Marc Russo: saxophones
Mic Gillette: trumpets, trombones
Cameron Stone: cello
Siedah Garrett, Dorian Holley, Nayanna Holley, Darryl Phinnessee, Amy Holland-McDonald, Gail Swanson, Tim James: backing vocals
Recorded primarily at Sunset Sound, Village Recorders, Studio D and John McFee's studio between 2007 and 2010
Produced by Ted Templeman
Released: 28 September 2010
Highest chart positions: US: 39, UK: did not chart

Almost ten years after *Sibling Rivalry* and nearly four decades on from their debut, *World Gone Crazy* finds The Doobie Brothers reuniting with producer Ted Templeman, the man behind their seminal 1970s run. The idea, it seems, was to reconnect with the sonic DNA of their golden years while acknowledging the passage of time. The result? A record that feels both reverent and renewed. Not quite a full-blown return to form, but certainly a confident shuffle in the right direction.

'We were getting ready for a tour at a rehearsal hall in LA,' Pat Simmons said in 2011, 'when, lo and behold, in walked Ted Templeman. He asked, 'Are you guys writing or doing any recording?' We said, 'We've been writing and *talking about* recording, but we haven't started.' We gave him some demos, and he came back and said, 'I love some of these tunes. Would you be interested in going in with me to lay down some tracks?' That was the beginning of the album. We went to John McFee's studio first, laid down a few tracks, then went to Sunset Sound, where I think we laid down 11 tracks in ten days.'

'Getting back together with Ted Templeman was pretty amazing', John McFee said in 2019. 'One thing that isn't at all unusual when working on a project is to have no idea what other people will make of it, and we get so inside of the process sometimes that it's impossible to have any real objectivity about it. When *World Gone Crazy* was mixed and sent for the audio mastering process, we were actually shocked at the reaction from the mastering lab. They were blown away, started bringing out the vintage mastering gear that they saved for 'special' projects, and we were surprised at the level of the positive reaction to the music; this kind of reaction continued when others and eventually the public heard the project. People really seemed to identify it with the old magic of the combination of Ted Templeman and the Doobie Brothers, so much so that it honestly caught us off guard a bit.'

World Gone Crazy isn't a desperate attempt to recapture past glories; it's an album by a band that know exactly who they are. There's swagger, yes, but also reflection; energy, but tempered by experience. Not every track lands, and a few feel like echoes of earlier triumphs, but there's sincerity throughout. A cameo by Michael McDonald is a cherry on top, reminding us of the range this band once had and still, occasionally, can tap into. Bill Payne is back on board as well, playing on six tracks.

The BBC's review was unduly harsh, however: The Doobie Brothers were not looking for new fans in 2010.

> The first Doobie Brothers album in ten years is a time capsule from the Nixon/Ford era. Working again with Ted Templeman, who produced their golden age of hits and West Coast anthems, they deliver a textbook set of what their borderline-superannuated fans want. Ageism is not cool, kids, but a glance at the accompanying retrospective DVD shows a lighting crew working ridiculously hard to veil the fact that the Doobies are now, shall we say, weathered. (Saga would consider them unsuitable cover stars.) It'd be absurd for them to discover a new dubstep/grime direction, so this is hoary bearded vintage boogie for people who found Lynyrd Skynyrd a little too experimental.
>
> Every song is sufficiently similar to their canon to give their people a rush of recognition. Electric and acoustic guitars play off each other, harmonies are honed; everything is so relaxed it makes The Eagles or Fleetwood Mac sound like Fucked Up [a Canadian hardcore punk band formed in 2001].
>
> Lead single 'Nobody' is actually a re-recording of a flop off their 1971 debut. It's a decent groove, albeit one you can envision Jeremy Clarkson shaking his jeans to. 'A Brighter Day' essays a reggae-soul lilt, while

'Chateau', ZZ Top-lite, turns the amps up to a risqué eight. The title track has these millionaires bemoaning 'tryin' to make my monthly rent'. It's a slick production, though the ill-conceived 'Young Man's Game' brags of '30 long years bringin' people rock 'n' roll' and disses 'those rock'n'roll critics talkin' yak yak yak'. Dudes, it's 40 years, and the critics forgot you half that time ago.

In the Doobies' heads and on this album, it's forever California 1974.

Is *World Gone Crazy* a classic? No. But it's solid, honest work from a band with nothing to prove and still something to say.

The vinyl version adds two bonus tracks and re-orders the songs thus:

Side one: 'A Brighter Day', 'Chateau', 'My Baby'
Side two: 'Don't Say Goodbye', 'Law Dogs', 'New York Dream'
Side three: 'Nobody', 'World Gone Crazy', 'Far From Home'
Side four: 'Young Man's Game', 'I Know We Won', 'Old Juarez', 'Little Prayer'

The band continued to tour throughout the 2010s, but Michael Hossack was diagnosed with cancer and was forced to leave the band after 25 years (second time around). He died in 2012.

'A Brighter Day' (Johnston)
The album opens in surprisingly buoyant fashion, with horns punching out bright stabs, percussion bubbling underneath and Tom Johnston striding in as if fronting a soul revue. This is Doobies-as-soul-band, harking back to the *Takin' It To The Streets* era, though here given a warmer Memphis polish and even a touch of calypso sway. Johnston's voice is lived-in, weather-beaten but stubbornly forceful, giving the anti-war lyric an edge it might not otherwise carry. Admittedly, the metaphor is heavy-handed – horrors of conflict translated into imagery a little too neat for comfort – but the optimism at its core is undeniable. The song radiates good cheer even while its words speak of darker themes, and that contradiction lends it more charm than it probably deserves. As an opener, it doesn't knock you backwards, but it sets a sunny tone, offering reassurance that the band can still conjure a groove that invites listeners in rather than daring them to resist. It's not a statement of intent so much as a friendly wave of recognition.

'Chateau' (Simmons, Templeman)
Pat Simmons slips into familiar territory with 'Chateau', a full-bodied boogie rocker that could almost have rolled off the cutting-room floor during their mid-1970s peak. The stop-start riffing is textbook Doobies-meaty chords, rhythmic drive and a bluesy vocal growl that instantly recalls the band's bar-band origins. It's comfort food, and Simmons knows it: nothing revolutionary, but precisely what fans expect and, truthfully, want. Lyrically, the song is

more enthusiastic than elegant. 'Standing on the back porch talking to your sister/The walls came down and hit me like a Twister' is unlikely to win any prizes for literary subtlety. But the groove is persuasive, the slide guitar authoritative and the piano rattles with real vigour. Ted Templeman's involvement as co-writer and producer ensures the sound is sharp and punchy, and the band clearly enjoy sinking their teeth into material that lets them stretch without over thinking. It's a solid, unpretentious rocker and one of the album's more convincing nods to their heritage.

'Nobody' (Johnston)

Released as a single in 2010. Charts: did not chart.

Revisiting the very first single they released in 1971, the Doobies risk both nostalgia and redundancy with *Nobody*. Yet, there's method to the decision. Pat Simmons: 'We wanted to reintroduce ourselves after being away for so long. It had the iconic sound we were known for, with the rhythmic guitars, finger picking and the harmonies we've employed throughout our career.'

The new version benefits from slick modern production – bright, balanced and fuller than the original – but loses none of its momentum. Tom Johnston's voice has aged considerably, its grain now more pronounced, but that roughness lends a kind of authority, a veteran still standing tall. Whether it improves upon the original depends on taste: the freshness of 1971 can't be recaptured, but the 2010 cut asserts the band's identity with conviction. Rather than a retread, it feels like a reclamation – a reminder of where they started and proof they still command the essentials of their sound.

'World Gone Crazy' (Johnston)

Released as a single in 2011. Charts: did not chart.

The title track marches in on a swamp-rock groove, dripping with bayou atmosphere. Johnston has long drawn inspiration from New Orleans, and in interviews, he openly acknowledged the debt to the city's giants: Professor Longhair, Allen Toussaint, the Neville Brothers, the Meters. 'It's a New Orleans feel', Tom Johnston explained to *Vintage Guitar* in 2011. 'This band has been influenced by that city a great deal... all those guys from New Orleans on the radio. Theirs was a very distinctive sound, like Stax/Volt had a very distinctive sound. I absolutely loved it. I wasn't aware where it was coming from. I didn't get to New Orleans until 1970, but when the band first played there, everybody was blown away by the music, the food, the feel of the town. You walk the streets or ride the streetcars out to those old type cemeteries, and everything's got Spanish moss hanging off of it... it's another world. And I'm still writing about it, so obviously, it had a huge impact.'

That heritage saturates this track, its syncopation and horns evoking the Crescent City with affectionate precision. Johnston's vocal, rough-edged yet deeply felt, delivers a lyric about societal decay – unrest, injustice, even a wrongfully accused delivery driver – strikingly blunt but undeniably heartfelt.

The chorus is simple yet effective, lodging itself firmly after only a couple of listens, while the band provide a muscular backdrop that never overwhelms the story. There's nothing subtle here, but there's conviction in every bar. In some ways, it's a companion to earlier social-consciousness moments in The Doobie catalogue, though this time filtered through the eyes of a seasoned observer rather than a wide-eyed idealist.

'Far From Home' (Simmons, Templeman)

Released as a single in 2011. Charts: did not chart.

One of the genuine highlights of their later career, 'Far From Home' finds Pat Simmons in reflective mode. It's a slightly wistful meditation on distance, memory and the human need for grounding, both in place and in relationships.

'It was not an obvious track to release as a single, in my opinion', he noted at the time. 'But I think it's one of the better songs I've written. We were pleasantly surprised that it charted [on the top 20 adult contemporary chart].

The video shows fan-supplied footage of real goodbyes and reunions. 'Doing the video was really cool, Simmons said. 'It was appropriately done and reflects the contents of the song. It's great to have a new album and some new music to perform for our audiences. We've been getting a great response to the songs in our set, and I feel we've added to our legacy and gained new fans along the way.'

Acoustic guitars set the mood, warm and enveloping, while the production is deliberately understated, resisting the temptation to over-orchestrate. The lyric is contemplative, tinged with regret and longing, and Simmons delivers it with a tenderness that comes only with experience. There's a hush to the track, a willingness to pause and let emotion fill the spaces between the notes. In an album often crowded with swagger and stomp, this song offers stillness, a quiet reminder that The Doobies are at their most affecting when they strip things back.

'Young Man's Game' (Johnston)

Irony alert: Tom Johnston declares 'It's a young man's game', while barrelling through this hard-rocking cut like he's Bob Seger in 1974. It's a hard-driving rocker that simultaneously admits to ageing and insists on defying it. The lyric plays with a familiar trope, the seasoned road warrior insisting he's still got fuel in the tank, and while the words themselves may lack imagination, the performance more than compensates. Guitars blaze, the piano hammers with relish and the rhythm section power forward as if daring anyone to call them past their prime. Johnston sings with a rasping determination, clearly relishing the contradiction. It's less about the message and more about the energy, proving that even if the years weigh heavily, the band can still sound convincingly youthful when they decide to let loose. A minor triumph, more convincing than it has any right to be.

'Don't Say Goodbye' (Simmons, Templeman)
And then, at last, Michael McDonald. He returns not just in name, but with that unmistakable voice, smooth and rich. The track itself is classic McDonald-era Doobies – lush chords, a lilting Latin groove and creamy production. Simmons sings lead and McDonald adds harmony and counterpoint vocals like old times. A lengthy harmonica and violin duel adds texture and surprise, stretching the song beyond formula. It's the kind of track that could only exist on a Doobies record: a mixture of boogie instinct, soulful harmony and adventurous polish. Nostalgic, certainly, but also alive in the present moment and a reminder of the band's unique ability to blend styles into something unmistakably their own.

'My Baby' (Johnston)
In contrast, 'My Baby' is the album on autopilot. Tom Johnston provides a straightforward blues shuffle, the band play it impeccably, and everyone goes home happy, but without much to remember. The lyric is particularly thin, leaning on clichés that wouldn't pass muster in even the most forgiving blues bar. Yet, the musicianship redeems it: the rhythm swings, Johnston's vocal still carries conviction and the ensemble perform with a polish that prevents it from being disposable. As a piece of craft, it's beyond reproach; as a creative statement, it adds nothing to the catalogue. One suspects it exists more as live filler than as an attempt at artistry.

'Old Juarez' (Johnston)
A clear nod – perhaps too clear – to Santana, 'Old Juarez' is drenched in Latin rhythms and guitar flourishes that unmistakably recall 'Smooth'. Tom Johnston's songwriting ensures the Doobie identity remains intact, but the resemblance is close enough to border on imitation. The irony is that both Santana and the Doobies emerged from the same late-1960s Bay Area stew, so the overlap is not unnatural.

Heard on its own terms, the track sparkles: crisp percussion, shimmering guitars and Johnston in commanding form. Through headphones, the detail of the production reveals itself – layers of rhythm and colour that make it far richer than its surface suggests. Derivative, yes, but undeniably effective.

'I Know We Won' (Nelson, Simmons)
Few collaborations arrive with the combined gravitas of Pat Simmons and Willie Nelson. Between them, decades of experience saturate 'I Know We Won', a country ballad that exudes calm assurance. The lyric is plainspoken but effective and both singers deliver with warmth and authority. The production is typically immaculate, letting the voices remain front and centre while the arrangement supports with tasteful restraint. There's nothing flashy here, no attempt to reinvent the wheel, but the song's very simplicity is its strength. It feels less like a bid for chart attention than a quiet affirmation of

shared musical roots. For fans, it's a pleasure simply to hear two veterans trading lines with such ease.

'Law Dogs' (Johnston)

Tom Johnston indulges his storytelling side with 'Law Dogs', a rollicking acoustic blues full of narrative detail. The lyric spins a pulp-tinged tale of jailbreaks, molls and desperadoes, the kind of material that might have fit on a roadhouse jukebox in the early 1970s. Musically, it's stripped back to acoustic slide guitars and a stomping rhythm, rawer than much of the surrounding album. The effect is both playful and cinematic, evoking dusty highways and neon-lit dive bars. Johnston may not be a novelist, but his ability to sketch a scene remains intact, and the band lean into the mood with relish. A lively diversion.

'Little Prayer' (Simmons)

Bonus track on vinyl album and 'deluxe edition' CD

'Little Prayer' is a gentle, almost fragile lullaby. Its opening recalls Radiohead's 'No Surprises' – a surprising touchstone – but the song itself is more in line with Pat Simmons' folksy, meditative instincts. Acoustic guitar and a soft vocal delivery carry the piece, while the lyric offers modest spirituality rather than bombast. There's humility in its tone, a willingness to speak quietly rather than shout. It adds a tender counterbalance to the album's more muscular moments, and though minor, it lingers.

'New York Dream' (Johnston)

Bonus track on vinyl album and 'deluxe edition' CD

A darker turn comes with 'New York Dream', a minor-key slice of soul-funk dedicated to the city that never sleeps. Horns lay down a tense foundation, while Tom Johnston intones his reflections with measured intensity. The arrangement is strong, full of colour and drive, and the song captures something of the urban atmosphere – restless, shadowed, alive at all hours. Lyrically, it doesn't break new ground, offering generalities rather than insight, but the performance sells it. As with much of the record, professionalism outweighs inspiration, yet the sound is so polished that it remains a pleasure.

'Delta Devil Dog' (McFee)
'Lie To Me' (Johnston)

Bonus tracks on the Japanese CD

Two curios added to the Japanese edition, these tracks showcase both the band's breadth and their workmanlike approach. 'Delta Devil Dog', a brisk 45-second instrumental, serves mainly as a showcase for John McFee's slide guitar prowess – short, sharp and entirely enjoyable. 'Lie To Me' offers the other end of the spectrum: a straightforward up-tempo blues with Johnston in familiar mode, rawer in production than most of the album, giving it a rough-and-ready charm. Neither adds much to the canon, but both are welcome glimpses behind the curtain.

Some editions also include 'Black Water' and 'Nobody', both recorded at Big Sky Studios in Ann Arbor, MI, for W-DET radio's long-running *Acoustic Café* programme.

Southbound (2014)

Personnel:
Tom Johnston: vocals, guitars
Patrick Simmons: vocals, guitars
John McFee: guitar, banjo, autoharp, fiddle, steel guitar, backing vocals
With:
Michael McDonald: vocals, keyboards
Zac Brown, Sara Evans, Tyler Farr, Eric Gunderson, Toby Keith, Stephen Barker Liles, Jerrod Niemann, Blake Shelton, Amanda Sudano-Ramirez, Chris Young: vocals
Casey James, Brad Paisley: vocals, guitar
Tom Bukovac, J. T. Corenflos, Vince Gill, Hunter Hayes, Dann Huff, Jerry McPherson: guitar
Jimmy De Martini: fiddle, backing vocals
Dan Dugmore: steel guitar, dobro
Shannon Forrest, Chris McHugh: drums
Larry Hall: violin, viola, cello, trombone, trumpet
Charlie Judge, Michael Rojas: keyboards
Huey Lewis: harmonica
Tony Lucido, Tommy Sims, Jimmie Lee Sloas: bass
Bryan Sutton: acoustic guitar, mandolin
Ilya Toshinsky: acoustic guitar, banjo, bouzouki, mandolin
Charlie Worsham: vocals, banjo
Clay Cook, John Cowan, Vicki Hampton, John Driskell Hopkins, Wendy Moten: backing vocals
Produced by David Lyndon Huff at Starstruck and Blackbird Studios, Nashville
Released: 4 November 2014
Highest chart positions: US: 16, UK: did not chart
Track listing: 'Black Water' (with Zac Brown Band), 'Listen To The Music' (with Blake Shelton and Hunter Hayes), 'What A Fool Believes' (with Sara Evans), 'Long Train Runnin'' (with Toby Keith and Huey Lewis), 'China Grove' (with Chris Young), 'Takin' It To The Streets' (with Love and Theft), 'Jesus Is Just Alright' (with Casey James), 'Rockin' Down The Highway' (with Brad Paisley), 'Take Me In Your Arms (Rock Me A Little While)' (with Tyler Farr), 'South City Midnight Lady' (with Jerrod Niemann), 'You Belong To Me' (with Amanda Sudano Ramirez and Vince Gill), 'Nobody' (with Charlie Worsham)

Little Feat's 2008 album *Join The Band* featured re-recordings of many classic tracks with guest vocalists such as Dave Matthews, Bob Seger, Vince Gill, Jimmy Buffett and Chris Robinson. *Southbound* operates from the same blueprint: take iconic American roots-rock, add guest stars (mostly from Nashville) and let the legacy shine through. Whereas *Join The Band* feels looser, more like a jam session with friends, *Southbound* is glossier, more produced and aimed squarely at the contemporary country market. 'I have to say that was one hell of a lot of fun', noted Pat Simmons. 'The studio musicians were incredibly good, easy to work with, enjoyable to hang out with and we always got the basic track in no more than two takes.' It was a risky manoeuvre: re-recorded hits rarely satisfy both purists and new listeners. So, does *Southbound* add depth to the Doobies' legacy or dilute it?

The album opens with a logical choice: Simmons' folky anthem 'Black Water' is given a gentle Southern facelift. Zac Brown's vocals blend easily with Simmons' laid-back drawl and the harmonies are rich without being syrupy. Musically, it stays close to the original, but the fiddle lines and subtle dobro remind you this is Music Row territory. It's respectful, well-executed and not without charm. Blake Shelton and Hunter Hayes re-imagine 'Listen To The Music' as a country-pop jam. Shelton is charismatic enough, but it's Hayes' guitar solo that impresses most – a flashy, fleet-fingered break that brings a bit of muscle to an otherwise sunny rendition. Still, the original's breezy swing is missed in favour of a more polished, almost radio-ready sheen. The reworking of 'What A Fool Believes' is a bold choice. Michael McDonald's Grammy-winning soft rock staple is re-cast as a duet with Sara Evans. She acquits herself well, matching McDonald's still-impressive vocal gymnastics with warmth and restraint. The arrangement is tastefully updated with pedal steel and light country twang. Toby Keith brings grit and Huey Lewis brings harmonica to 'Long Train Runnin''. The result is more bar-band boogie than country chart hit. It's heavier than the original, with a sharper edge to the guitars, and the chorus loses a bit of its syncopated swing. Still, it rocks, and the band clearly enjoy cutting loose. Chris Young adds gravitas to 'China Grove', Tom Johnston's tale of small-town weirdness. The riff remains untouched – wisely – and the backing band lean into the stomp. No reinvention here, just a well-oiled remake with a strong vocal. You miss the dirt of the original, but not by much. Love and Theft's shared vocals add a glossy country-pop flavour to 'Takin' It To The Streets', but the arrangement retains the original's gospel-tinged urgency, and Michael McDonald sings superbly. It doesn't have the original's bite, but it's slick and sincere. We have a fiery rendition of 'Jesus Is Just Alright', though one wonders how many of today's listeners know this was a cover even back in 1972. Casey James adds some vocal grit, but the track largely sticks to the original blueprint. The gospel backing vocals are a nice touch, and the band still attack it with conviction. Brad Paisley's appearance on 'Rockin' Down The Highway' is one of the album's high points, his signature Telecaster tone gliding effortlessly through Tom Johnston's rhythmic chug. This is what *Southbound* does best: a fresh coat of country lacquer on a classic car, but the engine still roars. 'Take Me In Your Arms (Rock Me A Little While)', The Doobies' Motown homage, gets a Nashville retread. Tyler Farr sings it well enough, but the energy feels somewhat restrained. The original's punch is slightly dulled by slick production; one wishes they'd leaned into the soul a little more. 'South City Midnight Lady' translates surprisingly well into modern country. Jerrod

Niemann's drawl adds a romantic weariness, and the pedal steel enhances the nocturnal melancholy. 'You Belong To Me' works brilliantly. It remains a smooth slice of jazz-pop, updated here with a delicate vocal from Amanda Sudano Ramirez (of Johnnyswim) and a marvellous guitar solo by Vince Gill. Michael McDonald returns to duet, and though the groove is looser, the spark remains. And finally, a nod to their earliest days, reimagining 'Nobody', the opening track of their debut album. Charlie Worsham lends a youthful vocal that's earnest and likeable, and the arrangement walks a line between swampy rock and polished country. It's a thoughtful close to a project steeped in self-reflection.

Southbound isn't essential listening for Doobie purists, but it's a far cry from cynical cash-in. The band sound engaged, the guest stars mostly add value and there's a genuine sense of celebration throughout. Some tracks err on the side of polite, but the musicianship is strong and the best moments feel like proper collaborations rather than exercises in nostalgia.

Live From The Beacon Theatre (2019)

Personnel:
Tom Johnston: vocals, guitars
Patrick Simmons: vocals, guitars, guitjo, banjo
John McFee: guitar, pedal steel guitar, dobro, violin, cello, harmonica, banjo, vocals
With:
John Cowan: bass, vocals
Ed Toth: drums
Bill Payne: keyboards, vocals
Marc Quinones: percussion, vocals
Marc Russo, Roger Rosenberg: saxophone
Michael Leonhart: trumpet
Recorded between 15 and 16 November 2018
Produced by The Doobie Brothers
Released: 28 June 2019
Highest chart positions: US: did not chart, UK: did not chart
Track listing: 'Listen To The Music', 'Rockin' Down The Highway', 'Mamaloi', 'Toulouse Street', 'Cotton Mouth', 'Don't Start Me To Talkin'', 'Jesus Is Just Alright', 'White Sun', 'Disciple', 'Snake Man', 'The Captain And Me', 'Natural Thing', 'Long Train Runnin'', 'China Grove', 'Dark Eyed Cajun Woman', 'Clear As The Driven Snow', 'Without You', 'South City Midnight Lady', 'Evil Woman', 'Busted Down Around O'Connelly Corners', 'Ukiah', 'The Captain And Me', 'Take Me In Your Arms (Rock Me A Little While)', 'Black Water', 'Listen To The Music (Reprise)'

Live From The Beacon Theatre presents live performances of *Toulouse Street* and *The Captain And Me* in their entirety. John McFee: 'This concept was something that had been floating around for some time, and we were finally able to schedule things so that we could prepare for this. We had had fans suggesting we do some kind of album-oriented type show, as well as discussion within the band, so it took hold, and while we were at it, it seemed like a good idea to capture it on film and audio, so the concept actually has become a reality. There was quite a bit of rehearsal involved in putting this concept together. There were songs, for example, that the band had never played live before, ever, and there were others that hadn't been part of a set for years or even decades, and so we had to do some serious homework. It was a lot of work, but it was also really rewarding and ultimately a lot of fun to play all the very cool material from those projects.'

Liberté (2021)

Personnel:
Tom Johnston: vocals, guitars
Patrick Simmons: vocals, guitars, guitjo, banjo
John McFee: guitars, mandolin, banjo, pedal steel guitar, backing vocals
With:
John Shanks: guitars, bass, dobro, keyboards, drum programming, percussion, backing vocals
Bill Payne: piano, Hammond B-3 organ, Wurlitzer organ, synthesiser
John Cowan: backing vocals
Victor Indrizzo: drums, percussion
Bob Glaub: bass
Jeff Babko: piano, synthesiser, Hammond B3 organ, Wurlitzer organ, clavinet
Bradley Giroux: drum programming
Lucy Woodward: backing vocals
Released on 1 October 2021
Produced by John Shanks
Highest chart positions: US: did not chart, UK: did not chart

When a band reaches its 50th anniversary – particularly one with a career as bifurcated and well-toured as The Doobie Brothers – you might expect a new studio album to be little more than a commemorative coaster: dutiful, deferential and quickly forgotten. *Liberté*, released in October 2021 after nearly a decade of silence, defies that assumption, if not quite overturning it.

Co-produced and co-written by John Shanks (Bon Jovi, Stevie Nicks, Van Halen, Bonnie Raitt, Miley Cyrus, Melissa Etheridge and enough contemporary rock acts to populate a cruise), *Liberté* was The Doobie Brothers' first full-length album of new material since *World Gone Crazy* in 2010. It's a modest, professional, well-executed collection of new songs from a veteran band that, despite half a century on the clock, still knows how to plug in, lock into a groove and deliver. There are no revelations here, but there's heart and there's effort. Both count for something. What's missing is risk. There's no 'China Grove', no 'South City Midnight Lady', no unexpected turns. This is the sound of a veteran band playing it safe, competently. Whether that's a comfort or a disappointment depends on what you wanted from your Doobies in 2021. As an entry in their discography, *Liberté* won't change anyone's life, but it won't embarrass the legacy either. And for a band 50 years in, that's no small thing.

During their time in isolation throughout 2020, the Doobie Brothers released at-home performances of 'Black Water', 'Listen To The Music' and 'Takin' It To The Streets' (with Michael McDonald). These performances can be found on their social media accounts, such as YouTube and Facebook. In addition, they collaborated with Dave Mason for a cover of Traffic's 'Feelin' Alright' and Peter Frampton for a cover of Eric Clapton's 'Let It Rain'.

The band's 50th anniversary tour commenced in August 2021, with Michael McDonald returning as a permanent member. By this time, *Liberté* had been completed, and therefore, McDonald did not take part. *Liberté* became the third Doobie Brothers album that failed to chart, after 2000's *Sibling Rivalry* and their 1971 debut.

'Oh Mexico' (Johnston, Shanks)
The album begins with the gently throbbing 'Oh Mexico', a tune that seems designed to ease listeners in rather than grab them by the collar. There's a hint of the travel brochure about the lyrics, with the sun-drenched images of tequila nights and lazy beach afternoons conjuring a world that feels closer to a package holiday commercial than the road-hardened boogie that The Doobies built their reputation on. Tom Johnston's voice, to its credit, remains remarkably resilient – weathered but strong, with a lived-in warmth that suits the material. The slide guitar cuts through with admirable clarity, offering the closest thing here to genuine dirt. Yet, the chorus, big though it is, doesn't quite catch fire. For an opener, it's curiously polite, as though the band were anxious not to scare off casual listeners. One misses the sense of abandon that *China Grove* provided in 1973, or the pure, unfiltered joy of *Listen To The Music*. Instead, we are presented with a track that's agreeable, accomplished, even handsome, but never quite dangerous enough to stir the blood.

'Better Days' (Simmons, Shanks)
Pat Simmons takes the wheel for 'Better Days', and immediately, the album feels brighter. Simmons has always been the Doobie most inclined toward reflection and a sort of laid-back optimism, and this mid-tempo shuffle is firmly in that tradition. The opening borrows more than a little from Springsteen's 'Secret Garden', but the chorus blossoms in familiar Doobie style, full of layered harmonies that nod to their prime years without descending into pastiche. There's sincerity here, too; Simmons has always sounded like he means what he sings, and the result is a track that feels heartfelt rather than manufactured. Lyrically, it's a gentle pep-talk, a reminder that tomorrow can indeed be better. The melody lodges itself more securely than most on the album. If Tom Johnston often leans on muscle, then Pat Simmons counters with warmth, and this song is one of the few moments where the balance feels just right. It doesn't rewrite the Doobie rulebook, but it proves Simmons still knows how to craft songs that resonate.

'Don't Ya Mess With Me' (Johnston, Shanks)
No surprises here: Johnston brings the stomp. 'Don't Ya Mess With Me' is an exercise in the kind of meat-and-potatoes boogie that has kept the Doobies' live shows rowdy for decades. A chunky riff, a chorus designed for shouting rather than singing and a bluesy vocal delivery that sounds like it was born in the barroom. It's brash, unsubtle and proud of it. Lyrically, it's all bluster and

bravado, the sort of chest-beating that was already old hat in 1973. But as with much of Johnston's work, it's less about the words than the *feel* – the crunch of the guitar, the steady stomp of the rhythm section and the sheer energy of the performance. One imagines it going down a storm in an outdoor amphitheatre, beers aloft, fists pumping. On record, however, its predictability is its weakness: the Doobies have done this sort of thing better, leaner and with more conviction in the past. Fun, certainly, but hardly essential.

'Cannonball' (Simmons, Shanks)
Simmons lightens the mood with 'Cannonball', a brisk and sprightly tune whose finger picked acoustic intro quickly gives way to a breezier tempo. There's an odd dissonance between the youthful buoyancy of the music and the fact that it's being sung by a man in his mid-60s, though in truth, Simmons still sounds remarkably fresh. The chorus, curiously enough, wouldn't be out of place on a Miley Cyrus record, full of pop sheen and youthful exuberance, but delivered here with an older man's genial smile. The production is pristine to a fault: every instrument polished to gleam, every harmony locked in place. For some, that immaculate gloss will be appealing; for others, it risks sanding off the quirks that once made The Doobies distinctive. Still, there's an undeniable charm in Simmons' delivery, and the song's sheer pep makes it one of the album's lighter, more enjoyable moments.

'Wherever We Go' (Simmons, Shanks)
The Doobies have long been masters of harmony, and 'Wherever We Go' leans heavily on that strength. Close vocal blends ride atop chiming guitars, creating a wash of sound that's instantly pleasing. The chorus aims for anthemic territory, with just a hint of late-period Bon Jovi about its stadium-sized ambition. Simmons, again, is the anchor, his voice still carrying a warmth and sincerity that makes even the most generic lyric feel genuine. There's a faint air of wish-fulfilment about the track, as though the band are trying to remind themselves as much as their audience that, wherever they go, they're still a unit worth following. It doesn't quite soar to the heights it reaches for, but it demonstrates the Doobies' knack for blending rock muscle with pop accessibility.

'The American Dream' (Johnston, Shanks)
Given its title, one might expect 'The American Dream' to deliver a bold statement, but in practice, it plays things curiously safe. Johnston sings of faded dreams and weary hearts, but the words are vague, more gesturing at themes than engaging with them directly. Musically, the song is tidy, almost too tidy, with polished production that undercuts the determination such a subject demands. There's some lovely slide guitar here, and Bill Payne's keyboards lend colour, but the track never quite commits to being either a political commentary or a personal lament. Instead, it hovers in the middle

ground, pleasant but empty. It's the kind of song that sounds fine while it's playing, but leaves little impression once it ends. A missed opportunity, perhaps, to say something more substantial.

'Shine Your Light' (Johnston, Shanks)
With 'Shine Your Light', Tom Johnston dials things back, offering a low-key, almost gospel-tinged ballad. It's hard not to hear echoes of 'People Get Ready' in both the sentiment and the melodic shape, though filtered through a Doobie-esque country-rock lilt. Johnston's voice is unusually restrained, almost tentative, but there's conviction in his delivery that grows as the song progresses. By the chorus, his voice rises into Springsteen territory, full of power and yearning. It's not a show-stopping number, but it does offer a glimpse of the band's more soulful instincts and serves as a refreshing change of pace from the more predictable boogie and gloss elsewhere on the record.

'We Are More Than Love' (Simmons, Shanks)
Earnestness can be both a blessing and a curse, and 'We Are More Than Love' sits squarely on the fence. The sentiment – unity, love, shared humanity – is impossible to argue with, yet the lyric often veers toward the sort of motivational-poster platitudes that feel more suited to a self-help seminar than a rock record. Musically, the chorus blooms with bright, clear harmonies, and the band play with absolute conviction. Simmons gives it everything vocally, his sincerity cutting through even when the words wobble under their own weight. The result is a track that will either strike listeners as uplifting or cloying, depending on their tolerance for grand gestures. At worst, it's saccharine; at best, it's a heartfelt, if slightly naïve, reminder of The Doobies' belief in music as a unifying force.

'Easy' (Johnston, Shanks)
Released as a single in 2022. Charts: did not chart.
'Easy' made no impact on the charts as a single, but it deserves a closer listen. Despite sharing a title with the Commodores classic, it owes more to Eric Clapton's 'Mainline Florida', to the point where 'tribute' feels like the most charitable description. Fortunately, Tom Johnston inhabits the song fully, delivering one of his strongest vocals on the record – rich, expressive and tinged with a weary sort of grace. The arrangement is atmospheric, letting the song breathe rather than forcing it into a rigid structure and the guitar work is beautifully restrained, adding texture without overwhelming the vocal. It's not revolutionary, but it's a late-career highlight that proves Johnston still has both the chops and the instinct for new music.

'Just Can't Do This Alone' (Johnston, Shanks)
This track flirts most directly with The Doobies' past, recycling the 'Long Train Runnin'' riff as its foundation. But Tom Johnston leans into it, delivering a

lyric about dependence and connection over a groove that hints at the band's funkier side. The chorus is undeniably catchy, with layered harmonies that recall their classic 1970s sound. Yet, the production – clinical, polished, almost antiseptic – robs the track of the raw energy it deserves. What could have been a rollicking funk workout is instead smoothed into something more radio-friendly, losing much of its bite. Still, there's a strong melody at its core, and Johnston sells the lyric with authority. A near miss, perhaps, but a miss nonetheless.

'Good Thang' (Simmons, Shanks)
Here, we drift into modern country territory, and the results are, at best, middling. 'Good Thang' is pleasant enough, with a sturdy backbeat and Simmons' easygoing vocal, but it feels generic, as though it could just as easily have been recorded by any number of Nashville acts. For a band once defined by their ability to fuse rock muscle with funk grooves and folk harmonies, this slide into glossy country feels like a retreat rather than an evolution. 'Good Thang' promises more, but the performance is almost too polite, lacking the edge or swing to justify its swagger. It's pleasant enough, but never quite dirty or funky enough to justify the title.

'Amen Old Friend' (Johnston, Shanks)
The album closes on a surprisingly intimate note with 'Amen Old Friend'. Tom Johnston sets aside the bluster and the boogie for a sparse, acoustic-led meditation, dedicated – one assumes – to the memory of late drummer Michael Hossack. The sentiment is genuine, the delivery unadorned and the result is quietly moving. There's no grand chorus, no glossy production, just a man singing farewell to a comrade. It stands in stark contrast to the polished surfaces elsewhere on the album and is all the more powerful for it. After a record of professional but often impersonal tracks, this closer provides a reminder of the Doobies' humanity. It's a dignified, understated exit and one of the album's few genuinely affecting moments.

Walk This Road (2025)

Personnel:
Tom Johnston: vocals, guitars
Michael McDonald: vocals, keyboards, accordion, acoustic guitar
John McFee: guitars, mandolin, harmonica, violin, cello, pedal steel guitar
Patrick Simmons: vocals, guitars, Dobro, keyboards, mandolin
With:
Mavis Staples: vocals
John Shanks: guitars, keyboards, mandolin, bass, banjo, percussion, background vocals
Victor Indrizzo, Mick Fleetwood: drums, percussion
Jeff Babko, Jamie Muhoberac: keyboards
Pino Palladino, Bob Glaub, Sean Hurley: bass
Woody Mankowski, Johnnie Bamont, Marc Russo: saxophones
Dean Parks: guitar
Jamie Hovorka, Marvin McFadden: trumpet
Mike Rinta: trombone
John Cowan, Sharlotte Gibson: background vocals
Jake Shimabukuro: ukulele
Henry Kapono: vocals
Released: on 6 June 2025
Produced by John Shanks
Highest chart positions: US: 76, UK: did not chart

Until their 50th anniversary tour, The Doobie Brothers' career could be divided into three distinct periods. Tom Johnston fronted the group from their formation in 1970, although his presence was minimal on *Takin' It To The Streets* (1976) and restricted to a guest appearance on *Minute By Minute* (1978). From 1975 to 1982, Michael McDonald – brought in during Johnston's illness – effectively took over as the creative centre, guiding the band toward a more polished, R&B-inflected sound. Johnston returned to lead in 1989, with McDonald reappearing sporadically: contributing as a guest performer to *World Gone Crazy* (2010) and *Southbound* (2014).

The idea of a full studio album uniting Johnston and McDonald had long intrigued fans. McDonald's *Wide Open* (2017) offered clues to what such a collaboration might yield: a voice deepened and enriched with age, exploring textures beyond his 1970s palette. Combine that with the most engaging elements of *Liberté* (2021) and – if producer John Shanks could enhance rather than dominate the sound – there was the possibility of a long-awaited resolution to a decades-old musical equation.

Walk This Road strides confidently along this stylistic tightrope, balanced with unexpected poise. The Doobie Brothers have never truly belonged to a single figure; they function best as a collective, each member contributing compositions that bear their own stamp. Producer John Shanks worked separately with each writer to build each song, and a different set of musicians would work on that song. The other Doobie Brothers add backing vocals, guitar or keyboards as necessary. All four of the Doobies only appear on two songs, but John McFee shines as a versatile utility player, here contributing resonator guitar, pedal steel, slide, mandolin, harmonica, violin and cello, each adding subtle colour to the arrangements.

Despite the fractured nature of the production, everything merges into a coherent, unified set. There is a shared enthusiasm in the project that belies the years of its creators, coupled with an acceptance that this might be the last lap around the block. 'It's an album of hope', Pat Simmons told *Hot Press* in 2025. 'The best things in life are free. Art and athletics, those are the things that have so much value; you don't have to think about the worst things in life that are going on. You can escape those moments.'

If *The Captain And Me* was the band in their glorious youth and *Cycles* was the sound of a comeback, then *Walk This Road* is The Doobie Brothers growing old with surprising grace – and still, somehow, finding new lines to draw on an old map. It's their best album since *Minute By Minute*. In retrospect, this first-ever collaboration between the band's three main songwriters feels both inevitable and long overdue. It's exactly the album that Doobies fans would wish for at this late stage in their career.

'Walk This Road' (McDonald, Shanks)

Opening the album, 'Walk This Road' finds Michael McDonald in notably fine voice, delivering a gospel-tinged lead that sets the tone for what follows. The track is unusual in featuring four lead singers in succession: McDonald, Tom Johnston (his voice now carrying an added rasp), Pat Simmons and, best of all, 85-year-old Mavis Staples, whose powerhouse delivery eclipses even her illustrious colleagues.

The arrangement is busy: weaving horns, John McFee's guitar slides and a rhythmic underpinning of funk-inflected syncopation and Latin and percussive touches nod to several strands of the band's past work. Lyrically, what might appear to be a straightforward celebration of friendship and reconciliation carries a more political subtext. McDonald told *Classic Rock* that the lyric reflects his concerns about the current state of American democracy, warning of the dangers of creeping authoritarianism and the importance of speaking out.

Inviting Mavis Staples was, in McDonald's words, 'kind of inevitable'. A long-time acquaintance, Staples has been an outspoken voice for social justice since the 1960s. Her contribution to the song underlines its intent, marrying R&B swagger with gospel fervour in a way that feels both timely and a touch radical.

'Angels & Mercy' (Simmons, Shanks)

Here, Pat Simmons' songwriting blends the finger picking style familiar from 'Black Water' with a more muscular arrangement, including a guitar solo that straddles bluegrass, blues and polished rock. The chorus feels slightly grafted-on, but the performance redeems it – particularly in the song's closing section, where guitars roar and McFee's fiddle soars above the mix. In the band's 2025 tour, this was a set highlight; those 'fans' heading to the bar missed one of the evening's strongest performances.

'Call Me' (Johnston, Shanks)
A concise, up-tempo slice of soul, 'Call Me' is as commercial as it is warmly executed. Tom Johnston's vocal is a model of understatement, and the lyric – a reminder that people are better together – needs no embellishment. The production is crisp, the arrangement uncluttered.

'Learn To Let Go' (McDonald, Shanks)
In which Michael McDonald pulls out one of the best songs of his career. It's poignant, soulful and offers sage advice: 'When you lose at love/This world may keep on turning/But it's just gonna keep on hurting/Till you learn to let go'. This song was released to social channels ahead of the album: it was the first new Doobie Brothers song to feature *that* voice for 45 years. It was worth the wait. Michael McDonald is still one of the best singers in the business, and on material like this, he is flawless. Track down the live version performed on *The Late Show* in January 2025: McDonald's falsetto will give you goose bumps.

'State Of Grace' (Simmons, Shanks)
Pat Simmons closes this sequence with a composition of easy grace and quiet confidence. Its lush arrangement and smooth vocal delivery disguise the craft beneath; it takes half a century of songwriting to make something this relaxed sound effortless. The chord changes are deceptively simple, but they're carefully chosen so that every shift feels inevitable. There's no wasted movement; every note leads naturally to the next, which is the hallmark of a songwriter who's spent decades internalising harmonic logic. The melody floats over the chords with a casual elegance, and Simmons sings with subtle dynamics, slight delays and tasteful pauses – the kind of nuanced phrasing that only comes from years of understanding how a voice interacts with a chord progression. The instrumentation never overplays. Guitar, keyboard, bass and percussion fill their spaces without crowding the song, letting the melody and harmony breathe.

'State Of Grace' is quite simply one of the best songs that this band has produced – it's a moving, astute, older-but-wiser reflection of being old enough to accept one's fate. There is a subtle religious undertone which is carefully articulated. Pat Simmons was 76 years old when 'State Of Grace' was released. Let's hope it's not his memorial.

'Here To Stay' (Johnston, Shanks)
If Pat Simmons is contemplating absolution on 'State Of Grace' as he edges towards life's final chapters, then Tom Johnston seems happily uninterested in

the notion. 'Here To Stay' opens in fine style with a burst of *a cappella* harmonies before settling into a robust, full-bodied – if not wildly original – slice of classic rock. Johnston's trademark vocal rasp remains gloriously intact, much as Michael McDonald's own silken tones have weathered the decades unscathed.

'The Kind That Lasts' (McDonald, Shanks)
This one could be parachuted into the Little Feat catalogue without raising an eyebrow: a swampy New Orleans backbeat, flourishes of Hammond and an incisive slide guitar part set the tone. The Doobies' links with Little Feat go back to 1972's *Toulouse Street*, where Bill Payne first appeared, contributing to most of their albums thereafter. Payne isn't on this recording – McDonald covers both keyboards and vocals, the sole Doobie in attendance – but the post-Lowell George Little Feat feel, particularly the Shaun Murphy era, is strong and appealing, if perhaps slightly at odds with its surroundings. The slide guitar and solo come courtesy of producer John Shanks.

'New Orleans' (Johnston, Shanks)
The title is apt: this has a muscular Rolling Stones swagger, sprinkled with Creedence Clearwater and a dash of rhythm and blues. Its infectious groove is topped by a concise, punchy guitar solo. Backing vocalist Sharlotte Gibson (whose CV includes Celine Dion and Mariah Carey) adds a gospel-tinged wall of sound that underlines the Stones influence – one can almost hear the ghost of 'Gimme Shelter' lurking in the corners. McDonald turns up here, too, on the accordion.

'Speed Of Pain' (McDonald, Shanks)
A brittle drum machine and vintage keyboard textures usher in McDonald's honeyed tenor. The arrangement builds gradually, drums and guitars joining to create a thoroughly modern sheen. McDonald's performance is superb, his voice rising to full force, though the song's tilt towards contemporary country feels more like a McDonald solo cut than a fully integrated band track.

'Lahaina' (McDonald, Simmons, Shanks)
Issued in November 2023, 'Lahaina' takes its name from the historic Maui town where Pat Simmons has lived for 25 years. The verses (likely Simmons' work) and the chorus (presumably McDonald's) mesh seamlessly. Fleetwood Mac's Mick Fleetwood, a fellow Maui resident, provides drums, joined by local musicians Jake Shimabukuro on ukulele – subtle in the mix – and Henry Kapono on backing vocals. Written in the aftermath of the 2023 wildfires, which destroyed Fleetwood's Front Street restaurant, the song is both a lament and an act of solidarity. As Simmons said at the time, 'When we wrote it, I was desperate to contribute something after the fires because I just felt so helpless.'

With its soulful, jazz-inflected groove, 'Lahaina' closes an album of remarkably high calibre. As John Aizelwood observed in *Classic Rock*: 'None of this should really work in 2025', noted John Aizelwood in *Classic Rock*. 'But the fact that The Doobie Brothers don't have to exist makes their actual existence all the more worthwhile, and *Walk This Road* is an album as full of joy as it is of craft. Sixteen albums in, they're still not letting themselves down.'

Concluding Thoughts: A Crossroads Of American Music

The Doobie Brothers emerged in 1970 in San Jose, California, at a moment when the counterculture was still vibrant, but rock was already fragmenting into myriad subgenres. Their earliest recordings, typified by 'Nobody' from their self-titled debut, bear the rough-hewn imprint of biker-bar rock, a music that owed as much to Creedence Clearwater Revival as to the burgeoning California sound. By their second album, *Toulouse Street* (1972), the group had refined their approach, and here the country-rock influence became more obvious. The hit single 'Listen To The Music' exemplifies this tendency: its acoustic strum, easy vocal harmonies and gently insistent rhythm encapsulate the optimism and communality that were hallmarks of early 1970s West Coast music. But there was always a harder edge to the Doobies. 'Rockin' Down The Highway', also from *Toulouse Street*, is a straight-ahead rocker, propelled by Tom Johnston's driving guitar. This duality – country-tinged warmth on one side, muscular rock on the other – would become a structural feature of their work.

By the time of *The Captain And Me* (1973), the Doobies had begun to stretch out. 'Long Train Runnin'', with its chugging rhythm guitar and syncopated groove, stands as a clear example of funk influence infiltrating their sound. It was a song rooted in jam sessions, and its rhythmic insistence marked the Doobies as a band capable of more than just sing-along choruses. Meanwhile, 'China Grove', also from *The Captain And Me*, demonstrates their penchant for myth-making within rock. Ostensibly a portrait of a quirky Texas town, it is driven by a muscular riff and showcases Johnston's gift for fusing humour with swagger. Already, one hears the seeds of the stylistic pluralism that would later define their Michael McDonald years.

The mid-1970s saw the band explore further textures. Pat Simmons' 'Black Water' from *What Were Once Vices Are Now Habits* (1974) is an excursion into Southern roots and bluegrass. Its fiddle, banjo-like guitar picking and swampy feel evoked the Mississippi Delta rather than the Bay Area. It was also their first number one single, proving that audiences were ready to follow the band into unexpected musical terrain.

The most radical genre shift in the Doobies' history came in 1975 when Michael McDonald joined the group, initially as a touring replacement for Tom Johnston. McDonald's influence swiftly reshaped the band's sound, infusing it with elements of soul, jazz and the smooth textures of what would later be termed yacht rock. 'Takin' It To The Streets' (1976) is emblematic of this era: a socially conscious lyric paired with a gospel-tinged vocal and chord changes that speak more to rhythm and blues than to country or rock. This transformation reached its apogee with 'What A Fool Believes' from *Minute By Minute* (1978). Co-written with Kenny Loggins, it remains the quintessential example of late-1970s sophisticated pop. Its polyrhythmic keyboard figures, falsetto vocals and tightly produced sheen placed the

Doobies in a lineage alongside Steely Dan and Hall & Oates, a million miles from the open-road strumming of 'Listen To The Music'. And yet, both songs are recognisably Doobie Brothers – a striking illustration of their remarkable adaptability.

With Michael McDonald, they bridged into the world of soul and jazz-influenced pop, aligning themselves with a broader shift in American music towards polish and sophistication. That they did so without alienating (or, at least, reducing) their audience speaks to their ability to reflect, rather than dictate, the changing currents of taste. In this sense, the Doobie Brothers serve as a microcosm of American music itself: restless, pluralistic and unafraid of reinvention. Few bands of their generation can claim to have succeeded in so many guises. They were not merely passengers on the journey of American popular music; they were co-drivers, steering the vehicle into new lanes while keeping one hand firmly on the wheel of tradition.

If one were to map the Doobie Brothers' catalogue onto a musical atlas, the lines would cover much of America. The band's reach is catholic in the best sense of the word: country-inflected strains surface in 'Slippery St. Paul', 'Disciple', 'South City Midnight Lady', 'Spirit', 'Black Water', 'Neal's Fandango' and 'Leave My Heartache Behind', while the later 'I Know We Won' and 'Can't Stand To Lose' keep company with them. Elsewhere, there are dabs of the blues in 'Snake Man' and 'Dark Eyed Cajun Woman'; the shimmering West Coast sound colours 'Clear As The Driven Snow' and 'Sweet Feelin''; and the confessional singer-songwriter mode is found in 'White Sun', 'Far From Home' and 'State Of Grace'.

Exotic touches abound. Reggae seeps gently into 'Mamaloi' and 'People Gotta Love Again', and the band occasionally stretch towards jazz-fusion: 'For Someone Special', 'Livin' On The Fault Line', 'Chinatown' and 'South Bay Strut'. They nod towards New Orleans in 'Keep This Train A-Rollin'', 'World Gone Crazy' and 'The Kind That Lasts', and Pat Simmons regularly provides acoustic palate cleansers such as 'Busted Down Around O'Connelly Corners', 'Slack Key Soquel Rag', 'Larry The Logger Two-Step' and 'Steamer Lane Breakdown'. Few outfits of their generation could essay a jazz instrumental like 'Flying Cloud' or dabble at the fringes of progressive rock so convincingly as on 'Daughters Of The Sea' and 'I Cheat The Hangman'. At other times, they edge perilously close to AOR ('I Can Read Your Mind', 'Too High A Price', 'Is Love Enough?').

Two strands, however, defined their character. The first was a streak of gospel-infused funk that energised 'Jesus Is Just Alright', 'Ukiah', 'Song To See You Through' and 'Wheels Of Fortune'. The second was their unabashed embrace of soul, tipping a hat to Motown and Stax through covers of 'Take Me In Your Arms (Rock Me)', 'Little Darling (I Need You)', 'Need A Little Taste Of Love' and 'One Chain (Don't Make No Prison)'.

And then, of course, there is the blue-eyed soul that became their calling card. Beginning with 'Takin' It To The Streets' and 'It Keeps You Runnin'', this vein runs through 'What A Fool Believes', 'Minute By Minute', 'Real Love' and beyond, marrying polish with genuine emotion. All of which sits comfortably alongside the band's more muscular rock excursions – 'Without You', 'Road Angel', 'The Doctor', '45th Floor' – which serve as reminders that, for all their musical wanderings, The Doobie Brothers never lost sight of the sheer thrill of volume and drive.

Their best-known songs, 'Listen To The Music', 'Long Train Runnin'', 'China Grove', 'Black Water' and 'What A Fool Believes', are not just hits; they are artefacts of different musical traditions, each absorbed and reinterpreted by a band whose very name has become synonymous with eclecticism.

*

To speak of The Doobie Brothers is to enter a rich tapestry of American music in the second half of the 20th century. This is not merely a band that scored a series of hits; rather, they stand as a prism through which the shifting sensibilities of the era can be refracted. Across their extensive back catalogue, The Doobie Brothers have been country rockers, blue-eyed soul men, purveyors of funk-infused pop and champions of roots-driven Americana. Their ability to move across genres while retaining a distinct identity is at once their strength and their defining contribution to American popular music.

To understand The Doobie Brothers is to recognise the fluidity of American music in the latter half of the 20th century. They emerged in the wake of the 1960s, when the boundaries between rock, country and folk were porous. They were quick to absorb the lessons of that openness. Their early embrace of country-rock placed them in the company of contemporaries like The Eagles and Poco, though the Doobies always retained a grittier, bar-band quality. They soon moved away to embrace many other types of American music.

The Doobie Brothers were never simply one thing. And therein lies their enduring appeal. In a popular music culture defined by hybridity and constant evolution, The Doobie Brothers exemplified the art of crossing borders without losing one's sense of home. Their story is not only one of commercial triumph and remarkable longevity but also of cultural resonance: a testament to the idea that the richest music often lies at the intersections.

In Memoriam

Cornelius Bumpus (saxophone, keyboards, vocals; 1979-1982, 1987, 1989-1990, 1993, 1995-1996)
Born: 7 May 1945 – Dallas, Texas. Died: 3 February 2004 – Sioux City, Iowa.

John Hartman (drums, vocals; 1970-1979, 1987-1991)
Born: 18 March 1950 – Falls Church, Virginia. Died: 29 December 2021.

Michael Hossack (drums; 1971-1973, 1987-1991, 1993-2012)
Born: 17 October 1946 – Paterson, New Jersey. Died: 12 March 2012 – Dubois, Wyoming.

Keith Knudsen (drums, vocals; 1973-1982, 1987, 1993-2005)
Born: 18 February 1948 – Le Mars, Iowa. Died: 8 February 2005 – Kentfield, California.

Bobby LaKind (percussion, vocals; 1976-1982, 1987-1989)
Born: 3 November 1945 – New York. Died: 24 December 1992 – Los Angeles, California.

Chet McCracken (drums, vibraphone, marimba; 1979-1982, 1987)
Born: 20 September 1946 – Tacoma, Washington. Died: 11 February 2022 – West Hills, California.

Dave Shogren (bass, keyboards, guitar, vocals; 1970-1971)
Born: 12 October 1950 – San Francisco, California. Died: 14 December 1999 – San Jose, California.

Bibliography

Bego, M. , *The Doobie Brothers: Behind The Scenes With Today's Hottest Group* (Fawcett Popular Library, New York, 1980).
Frame, P. , *Rock Family Trees Volume 2* (Omnibus Press, London, 1983).
Johnston, T. and Simmons, P. with Epting, C. , *Long Train Runnin': Our Story* (St. Martin's Press, New York, 2022).
McDonald, M. with Resner, P. , *What A Fool Believes: A Memoir* (HarperCollins, London/New York, 2024).
Simon, C. , *Boys In The Trees* (Macmillan, New York, 2015).